D1596766

RUSSIAN AND EAST EUROPEAN STUDIES

Revolution

IN PERSPECTIVE

MORAVIA

CZECHOSLOVA

0 20 40 60   MILES
0 20 40 60 80   KILOMETERS

Danube

Morava

Vág (Vah)

Vienna

Pozsony
(Bratislava)

Ipoly

L. Neusiedl

Komarno

Vác

Sopron

Raba

Györ

Budapest

Szombathely

HUNGARI

Graz

STYRIA

Mur

L. Balaton

SOVIET

Klagenfurt

Drava

Maribor

Czaktornya

Nagykanizsa

REPUBLI

Ljubljana

Szigetvar

Barcs

Pécs

Baja

Szeged

CARNIOLA

Zagreb

Mohács

Danube

Szabadka
(Subotica)

Rijeka
(Fiume)

CROATIA

SLAVONIA

Osijek

Drava

Novi Sad

Y U G O S L A V I A

Sava

ADRIATIC SEA

Una

Banja Luka

BOSNIA

Vrbas

Bosna

Drina

DALMATIA

Sarajevo

Przemysl

GALICIA

Stryj

Uzhok Pass   Stanislav

(Uz)

Dniester

Kassa
(Košice)

Ungvár
(Uzhgorod)

Chernovtsy

Tisza

RUTHENIA

Miskolc

Maramarossziget
(Sighet)

BUKOVINA

Szatmár-Németi
(Satu-Mare)

Debrecen

Nagykaroly
(Carei)

NEUTRAL ZONE March 20, 1919

Szamos

Moldava

Nagyvárad
(Oradea)

Bistrița

MOLDAVIA

örös

Békéscsaba

Kolozsvár
(Cluj)

Targu-Mures
(Marosvásárhely)

Arad

TRANSYLVANIA

R O M A N I A

Temesvár
(Timişoara)

Maros (Mureş)

Olt

Nagyszeben
(Sibiu)

(Timiş)

BANAT

Beograd
(Belgrade)

Danube

Turnu-Severin

S E R B I A

HUNGARIAN SOVIET REPUBLIC	
March–July 1919 (approximate area)	‖‖‖
1914 boundaries, Hungary and adjacent nations	▬ ▬ ▬
1918 armistice lines	– – –
1971 national boundaries	▬▬▬
December 1918, Romanian occupation	⧅
January 1919, Yugoslavian occupation	⧄

Revolution

IN PERSPECTIVE

Essays on the
Hungarian Soviet Republic of 1919

Edited by Andrew C. Janos and William B. Slottman

University of California Press, Berkeley, Los Angeles, London
1971

University of California Press
Berkeley and Los Angeles, California
University of California Press, Ltd.
London, England

Copyright © 1971, by
The Regents of the University of California

Library of Congress Catalog Card Number: 74–138510
International Standard Book Number: 0–520–01920–2
Designed by James Mennick
Printed in the United States of America

Contents

Preface

CELEBRATING the anniversaries of great events or the birthdays of great men has become one of the major intellectual and social pastimes of the academic community. In honor of each occasion a conference is held, scholars are asked to indulge in a mixture of nostalgia and analysis, and a book is usually produced that presents the papers and comments made upon them by those attending the celebration. Such occasions are often memorable for reasons not strictly academic. Tragic or comic stories are told of the scholars who fail to appear, of papers that do not arrive on time, of discussions that become too polemical, and of social events that wander from the solemnity appropriate to the occasion.

Scholars specializing in the history and politics of the area once embraced by the Habsburg monarchy have been particularly prone to indulging in this pastime. In recent years they have had abundant reason for doing so, since in a few years they have been able, indeed expected, to remember the *Zusammenbruch* of 1918, the emergence of the newly independent states of Austria and Czechoslovakia, and the peace treaties signed in various Parisian suburbs that had some bearing on the fate of the Danubian peoples. In addition, they also had to mark anniversaries that went back one hundred years to Königgrätz and the establishment of the Dual monarchy. For scholars with the requisite time and energy it was possible to be constantly in movement, as one after another anniversary rolled around with almost frightening frequency.

When we first entertained the idea of holding a conference that would mark the proclamation of the Hungarian Soviet Republic on March 21, 1919, we were conscious that we might be risking an expression of apathy on the part of many scholars in this field. We knew that there had been too many anniversaries, and we were also aware that this particular one had its ambiguities. The 133 days of the Kun regime had not given it a well-defined niche in history, and it continued to appear to be episodic or parochially Hungarian. The regime had not suffered from a bad press but rather from a desire of its would-be chroniclers to turn to other and more attractive events. The reasons for a lack of interest in Hungary were obvious enough and respectable enough; the reasons for a similar lack of interest outside of Hungary were not. But Western Europeans and Americans might be forgiven for not turning with enthusiasm to men who had not made an impressive mark on history, had not been particularly distinguished as political figures or attractive as human beings, and who had not even been fortunate enough to make a major contribution to the folklore of world revolution.

This apathy and absence of a large scientific literature did suggest that a conference of the kind we envisaged might be of some use. If we could bring together scholars with more than the usual degree of polite interest in our theme and present papers that would elicit real discussion on the part of all participants, we could add to the general store of information and present the Hungarian Soviet Republic without making a claim for completeness or for providing a comprehensive reevaluation of the regime. The papers presented at the Berkeley Conference on March 21–22, 1969, tried to break new ground by approaching selected issues of political history but maintaining a certain balance between internal and external affairs as well as between the antecedents and the impact of the revolutionary events. One of the papers presented and published here dealt with the origins of the revolution: Andrew C. Janos in his "Decline of Oligarchy: Bureaucratic and Mass Politics in the Age of Dualism, 1867–1918" attempted to explore connections between the Soviet Republic and the previous history of Hungarian politics and society. Two papers were devoted to the internal political history of the regime: Peter Kenez's "Coalition Politics in the Hungarian Soviet Republic" and Andrew C. Janos's "The Agrarian Opposition at the National Congress of Councils" hoped to remove some of the mystery that had been allowed to collect around the political structure of the Kun regime. Another two essays examined the record of the Republic from the vantage point of Hungary's neighbors to the east and the west. Keith Hitchins studied the reactions of the Rumanians in Transylvania "The Rumanian Socialists and the Hungarian Soviet Republic," and the reactions of the grandees of Austrian culture to contemporary events in Hungary are discussed by William Slottman in "Austria's *Geistesaristokraten* and the Hungarian Revolution of 1919." Richard Löwenthal's "Revolution in Perspective" completes the series of articles by establishing links between the events in Hungary and the subsequent history of Communism.

In presenting these articles in book form we must express our gratitude to the Center for Slavic and East European Studies of the University of California for a grant that made the conference and this book possible. We wish to thank the scholars who joined us on that occasion for their company, their enthusiasm for our theme, and the suggestions they made to those who presented the papers. We should like to express our special thanks to Professor David

C. Hooson, the Chairman of the Center, for his many kind-nesses, and to its Secretary, Mrs. Eileen Grampp, for all she did to organize the conference and to assist us in preparing these articles for publication.

A. C. J.
W. B. S.

The Decline of Oligarchy
Bureaucratic and Mass Politics in
the Age of Dualism (1867-1918)

Andrew J. Janos

IN THE broadest sense this first chapter is addressed to the *ancien régime* overthrown by the revolutions of 1918–1919. More explicitly, it examines the structure and disintegration of the pre-1918 political system and the rise of centrifugal forces in Hungarian society that eventually led to the upheavals in the wake of World War I. What was the character of the old regime and what conditions explain its demise? These are the main questions that this chapter sets out to answer.

Beyond their immediate relevance to the subject matter of this book, its themes have been selected because of some dissastisfaction with the way in which Hungarian historiography, both Marxist and nationalist (as well as pre-Marxist radical), has traditionally treated them. Irrespective of ideological bent, major histories of the so-called Age of Dualism (or Compromise Era) tend to commit the same fundamental error; they view the history of Hungary from the perspective of categories derived from the unique experiences of a handful of Western societies, above all from those of Britain, France, and Germany. Not surprisingly has had debilitating consequences for empirical research. these categories often fail to fit Hungarian reality, which Frequently significant aspects of social and political relations have been ignored merely because of the lack of obvious analogies with patterns in the history of the West. In other instances, facts have been stretched to fit a preconceived framework, or even worse, the use of convenient labels has taken the place of empirical research. These tendencies have led to the widespread application of such terms as "feudal," "traditional," or "feudal-capitalist," in describing the character of the political regime, and were partly responsible for the standard image of Hungary ruled by a landed aristocracy under governments insensitive to modern ideas and the hard realities of socio-economic change. Curiously enough, in this respect there is hardly any difference between such conservative critics of the regime as Gyula Szekfü [1] and the more recent castigators of the Age of Dualism.

The purpose of this discussion is not to refute but to modify this image. For one, there will be no attempt here to deny the continued and disproportionate influence of the landed classes, nor the political survival of groups that had been part of the pre-1848 feudal institutional order. On the other hand, it will be necessary to argue for the growing differentiation of the ruling classes, and to point out the ascendancy of a bureaucratic machine that became an interest group in its own right and, for reasons of self-preservation, responded vigorously to the social, economic, and political imperatives of modernization often in conflict with the in-

---

[1] See especially the generally accepted conservative critique of Hungarian politics in the era of the compromise, Gyula Szekfü, *Három Nemzedék* (Three Generations), (Budapest: Egyetemi Nyomda, 1920).

terests of the landed classes. In this respect, one should further point out, the Hungarian experience was different
from the better-known Western models of modernization,
but similar to the experiences of contemporary "emerging
nations" struggling, as Hungary did in the nineteenth century, to overcome the psychological and material handicaps
of backwardness and belated development.

If problems of structure and performance raise questions of interpretation, then political disintegration (the
second half of our subject) raises questions of conceptualiza-
tion as well. Complex political change, of course, may be
analyzed intuitively, yet much is to be said for a more sys-
tematic approach that may lead us onto new paths of inquiry. Thus we will discuss the crisis of Hungarian politics
from the perspective of "social mobilization" and "political
development," two categories that have emerged from recent writings in political sociology as well as from empirical
studies of the politics of contemporary "developing" nations. The first one of the pair, "mobilization," relates to
the growing political awareness and "relevance" of wider
social strata as they break away from a traditional way of life
and emerge as a "public" available for sustained political
activity and commitments. This process is the result of such
aspects of modernization as literacy, exposure to mass communications, and changing forms of economic organization.
Social mobilization occurs when "large numbers of people
[are] moving away from a life of local isolation, traditional-
ism and political apathy, and [are] moving into a different
life of broader and deeper involvement in the vast complexities of modern life, including potential and actual involvement in mass politics." [2] Mobilization releases new
political forces and calls for adaptations on the part of the

2 Karl W. Deutsch, "Social Mobilization and Political Development,"
The American Political Science Review, LV:3 (1961), 494.

political system, the most significant of these being "development," that is, the incorporation of the rising strata into an institutional framework for mass politics.[3] Development in this sense is not identical with democracy, but it does imply the recognition of social diversity, the routinization of give-and-take, and the establishment of standard procedures (such as elections) that by themselves are capable of legitimating public policy.

Though we often use the term "developing" in connection with many countries of the contemporary world as if anticipating a particular outcome, the evidence suggests that we deal with a precarious process, fraught with dangers and contingent upon a number of conditions. In general terms, development appears to depend on the successful absorption and incorporation of newly mobilized strata into the status and reward system of society. To put it in different words, in order to develop politically a society must provide, by autonomous adaptation or conscious design, economic benefits and new avenues of mobility to large numbers of people, above all to those who acquire new political skills and competence through exposure to modern education. This in turn depends on the subjective condition of the "openness" of the old elites, their receptivity to new social groups and modern political symbols (especially to symbols emphasizing equity in social recruitment and the distribution of social values),[4] and on the objective con-

---

[3] This concept of "development" was first elaborated in Samuel P. Huntington, "Political Development and Political Decay," *World Politics*, XVIII:2 (1965), 386–430.

[4] The notion that equity is a fundamental aspect of modern legitimacy, and hence of development, is generally accepted in contemporary political writing, and forms one of the central ideas of a project on development sponsored by the Committee on Comparative Politics of the American Social Science Research Council. For discussions of the subject see Lucian W. Pye, *Aspects of Political Development* (Bos-

dition of material resources that set limits to consumption, social services, and the number of high status positions that the system can provide. As a corollary one may also hypothesize that the success of political development depends on a continued favorable balance between social mobilization and economic growth, or the rate at which society is capable of producing material resources and new forms of wealth.

The politics of social mobilization therefore is not always the politics of development. As the gap widens between aspirations and fulfillment, between demands and resources, the effectiveness of the government will be in jeopardy unless bolstered by repression. But since traditional oligarchies, autocracies, and bureaucratic polities are notoriously weak on this score, being restrained by habits and covenants that sustain their legitimacy, the outcome of mobilization will be more frequently political stagnation or decay. The government of a modernizing society will often find itself in a vicious circle: Economic limitations breed ineffectiveness, ineffectiveness breeds popular contempt, which in turn further lessens the chances of overcoming economic disabilities. The next stage may be anarchy or revolution from which eventually a new elite may arise possessing the skills of mass communication, organization, and repression, and capable of rallying the mobilized strata of society around grandiose schemes of social change and utopian visions of the future. This is a frequent pattern for political change in the modernizing countries of our days and, in brief, this is also the story told on the following pages and in the later chapters of the book.

Our story of the old regime must start with the *Ausgleich* or Compromise of 1867, the act of reconciliation be-

---

ton: Little, Brown, 1966), pp. 45-47. Also, David E. Apter, *The Politics of Modernization* (Chicago: University Press, 1965), pp. 1–43.

tween the house of Habsburg and the Hungarian political nation. This act ended nearly two decades of autocratic government and settled Hungary's relations with the Crown as well as with the rest of the Habsburg realm. In short, this document restored the domestic autonomy of the country while specifying that foreign relations and defense (as well as finances pertaining to them) were to remain "common affairs" and designating customs, commerce, and fiscal policies as "affairs of common concern" for the Austrian and Hungarian governments. The emperor of Austria was to be crowned the king of Hungary, enjoy the traditional prerogatives of Hungarian royalty, and act as the commander-in-chief of a common Austro-Hungarian army.

The Compromise restored constitutional government that had its origins in the Middle Ages but had been subjected to overhaul in 1848. It now provided for Cabinet government responsible to the two houses of parliament. One of these was a House of Lords whose membership, with some exceptions, was hereditary. Politically more significant than the lords was the House of Representatives returned by an electorate that included approximately 6 per cent of the population. Although the legal and political rights of commoners had been recognized in 1848, political practices and ingrained habits favored the traditionally "established classes," the aristocracy and the lesser nobility [5] (now commonly referred to as the "gentry"), and ensured their continued public prominence. Throughout the entire period members of these classes dominated the Cabinet [6] and the

---

[5] In Hungarian law and custom a formal distinction existed between a titled aristocracy (barons, counts, and dukes) and a "common" or untitled nobility. In 1842 the former included 169 families, the latter comprised an estimated 135,000 families or approximately 5.5 per cent of the population.

[6] A list of all Hungarian cabinet ministers appears in Hungarian Royal

House of Representatives. In the latter, in 1869 the gentry
and the aristocracy [7] comprised 69.4 per cent of the membership (56.1 and 13.3 per cent respectively), in 1872, 77.4
per cent.[8] Thereafter the grip of the traditional classes over
parliament began to slip. But as late as 1910, 58.4 per cent
of the representatives still belonged to one or the other
estate of the nobility (42.4 per cent to the gentry and 16 per
cent to the aristocracy).[9]

The presence of the gentry was even more evident in
the newly created system of public administration. When
constitutional government was restored, tens of thousands
of the offspring of gentry families applied for positions and
the governments of the day took a sympathetic view of their
plight. Under Kálmán Tisza's premiership it became official
policy to favor the gentry in bureaucratic recruitment, and
by the end of Tisza's long years in office, the common nobility were firmly entrenched in all branches of the civil service. In 1890 more than two-thirds (67.5 per cent) of the
senior officials (*fogalmazói kar*) in the Office of the Prime
Minister were of gentry origin. In the Ministry of the Interior this figure was 64.1 and even in the less exclusive De-
partment of Finance it was 53.8 per cent. The proportion

Office of Statistics (Magyar Királyi Statisztikai Hivatal), *Magyarország
Tiszti Cím és Névtára* (The Directory of Official Hungary), (Budapest: Magyar Király i A'llami Nyomda, 1938), pp. 4–7. Titles of nobility are either indicated or can be checked against information in
Béla Kempelen, *Magyar nemesi családok* (Hungarian Noble Families), I–VI (Budapest: Grill, 1911–1936).

[7] Hungarian constitutional law, unlike British, did not bar peers from
membership in the lower chamber.

[8] Ernö Lakatos, *Magyar politikai vezetöréteg, 1848–1918* (Hungarian
Political Elites, 1848–1918), (Budapest: Élet Nyomda, 1942, pp. 26
and 46.

[9] Based on Ferenc Végváry and Ferenc Zinner, *Országgyülesi Almanach*
(Parliamentary Almanac), (Budapest: Pázmáneum, 1910), and Kempelen, *op. cit*

of the gentry was even higher in local administration: 48
out of the 64 chief administrative officers (*alispán*) of the
counties came from gentry families, three of them from the
titled aristocracy.[10] "In the seventies and eighties," writes
one social historian of the period, "the best letter of recom-
mendation for an administrative career was a noble name.
. . . At first came the impoverished members of illustrious
families, then the petty *noblesse* and ultimately the educated offspring of the beggar (*bocskoros*) nobility." [11] Thus although the numerical preponderance of these groups continued to be a conspicuous aspect of public life, the profile
of the politically active nobility had undergone considerable transformations. Before 1848 the typical public figure
was not only a nobleman but also the owner of considerable
tracts of land. At the National Assembly of 1848 and the
short-lived diet of 1861 prosperous country squires were
still supreme in number and influence,[12] but after 1867 the
trend was reversed and in the last quarter of the nineteenth
century only about one-third of all deputies in the lower
house were land-owners. Most deputies now came from occupational groups more characteristic of modern, urban-
ized societies. Approximately one-fourth of the membership
of the House of Representatives were lawyers, one-fifth of
them qualified as "freelancers" (active in writing, journalism, and the arts), and a substantial number of them came
from the civil service into parliamentary life (Table I).

In the last quarter of the nineteenth century, the gentry was not only prominent among office holders but also

---

[10] *Magyaroszág Tiszti Cím és Névtára* (Budapest: Királyi Statisztikai
Hivatal, 1890) .

[11] Zoltán Lippay, *A magyar birtokos középosztály és a közélet* (The
Hungarian Landed Middle-Class and Public Life) , (Budapest: Frank-
lin, 1919) , p. 98.

[12] Lakatos, *op. cit.*, p. 49.

among the electorate. The franchise laws of 1848 and 1874
established an economic and educational census for voting
—the ownership of one-quarter session of land (approximately 7 to 10 acres), in urban areas the ownership of a

Table I. Occupational Distribution in the House of
Representatives, 1892 and 1901 (in percent)

Year	land-owners	profes-sionals*	Free-lancers	Bureau-crats	Business	Other
1892	37.5	25.7	9.3	18.1	5.8	3.6
1901	31.7	29.0	11.1	18.3	3.9	6.0

*Includes lawyers, doctors, pharmacists.
Source: Rezsö Rudai, "Adalék a magyar képviselöház szociológiá-
jához, 1887–1931" (Notes on the Sociology of the Hungarian House of
Representatives, 1887–1931), *Társadalomtudomány*, XIII (1933), 215–
230.

house or the payment of 10 florins in direct taxes, or else ten
years of education or more—but exempted members of the
petty nobility from them by stipulating that anyone whose
family name had appeared in any of the voting registers before 1848 (when only noblemen had the right to vote) would
be entitled to cast a ballot by "ancestral right" irrespective
of property or educational qualifications. These bills gave
the country an electorate of about 700,000 including 5.8 per
cent of the total population in 1874. In the same year, 168,-
921 voters or almost one-fourth of this electorate took advantage of this clause. In Transylvania where a special
census had been adopted to exclude all but 3.2 per cent of
the population, the impoverished gentry, with 80,896
votes, made up 66 per cent of the electorate.[13] In the subsequent years the number of voters by "ancestral right" de-

---

[13] *Annuaire Statistique Hongrois*, VIII (1900), 389. Also Hungary
Parliament: House of Representatives Országgyülés: Képviselöhaz),
Napló (Proceedings), XI (1874), 343.

clined as the gentry entered the professions and the
bureaucracy and began to register under different clauses of
the electoral law. (It was only 48,201 in 1901 and 22,908 in
1910.)[14] But throughout these years their class played a significant role in electoral politics, a role that was even more
pronounced because of the relative apathy and inexperi-
ence of the rest of the electorate.

However, the gentry's public prominence and political
weight was not primarily due to numbers but to organization, specifically to their hold over the system of public administration. With the levy and collection of new taxes, the
issuance of licenses and the regulation of rural life by scores
of ordinances, the bureaucracy began to loom large in the
village. The gendarme, the tax collector, and the chief notary (the head of the village administration) gradually sup-
planted the local squire in the lives of many rural inhabitants. Emancipated from the tutelage of the feudal landowner, the independent smallholder was now under the
sway of officialdom; and since peasant farmers made up the
bulk of the voters in the countryside, the electoral process
became vulnerable to administrative pressure and subver-
sion, giving the bureaucracy a powerful leverage over parliamentary politics.

Electoral corruption—the purchase of votes and the
use of forgery and intimidation—had been known in Hungarian politics before, but in the last quarter of the nineteenth century such methods of influencing elections became routinized and institutionalized. Under the premiership of Kálmán Tisza a large number of "rotten boroughs"
were created virtually under the bureaucratic tutelage.
From 1875 on in approximately 160 constituencies (out of
a total of 413)[15] candidates of the incumbent party were

---

14 *Annuaire Statistique Hongrois*, XIX (1911), 438.
15 See Ferenc Fodor, "A magyar képviselöválasztások térképe, 1861–

returned with monotonous regularity, frequently without opposition. These districts, inhabited mainly by Slovaks, Rumanians, and other national minorities, were treated by the governments of the day as so many feudal fiefs to be granted as patrimonies to the personal entourage of the prime minister (the so-called Mameluke Guard) or to candidates favored by high officials in public administration. Through this device Tisza integrated the now centralized bureaucracy with the parliamentary Liberal party thereby laying down the foundations of a political machine that was to occupy the center of the stage until the end of the period. While the bureaucracy was used to "make" elections and to ensure the perpetuation of the Liberal majority, the latter became the chief representative of public administration in parliament providing an aura of legitimacy to bureaucratic policies and interests. This arrangement did not lack an element of reciprocity and bargaining, and the machine had none of the single-minded ideological devotion of modern totalitarian organizations, yet it enabled the premiers of Hungary to maintain continuity of purpose and policy. Above all, it strengthened the position of the government vis-à-vis the Crown and the Austrian half of the monarchy and acted as an instrument of maintaining Magyar supremacy in domestic politics by effectively excluding Slovak and Rumanian voters from political participation.

This machine obviously dominated but did not monopolize national politics. Far from being a model autocracy, the political system permitted the representation of diverse economic interests. Most conspicuously, the economic weight of the *latifundia* was taken into account in

---

1915" (The map of Hungarian parliamentary elections, 1861–1915) in Hungarian Ministry of Foreign Affairs, *Hungarian Peace Negotiations: The Hungarian Peace Delegation in Neuilly* (Budapest: Hernady, 1922), IIIB, Annex VII.

both houses of parliament. In the upper chamber landed interests were represented directly, though the powers of the peers were now considerably shorn by law and custom. More significant was the indirect influence of the aristocracy over the House of Representatives where 50 to 70 seats were virtually at the disposal of the large estates. The electorate of these constituencies consisted mainly of the tenants and clients of a single large landowner whose economic influence in the village outweighed the administrative leverages available for local officials. Some of the patrons of such boroughs would sit in the House of Representatives themselves (there was, one should remember, no ban on the election of peers to the lower chamber) others merely sent their lawyers and bailiffs to represent them while they would take their seat in the House of Lords. In other instances, as had been the custom in Britain before 1832, such constituencies were open to young men of talent or else the constituencies would be up for sale. This practice, decried as the system of "old corruption" by a democratic century was beneficial in its own time in that it permitted the representation of urban wealth apart from the bureaucracy and aristocracy.

The rest of the constituencies, 180 to 200, were "open" for electoral contests or at least for competition among several groups of local notables outside the bureaucracy. Most of these boroughs were situated in the Magyar-inhabited areas of the Great Plain and in eastern Transylvania where the local gentry and a Protestant smallholding class was independent-minded and stubborn enough to resist bureaucratic encroachments on their political rights. Thus although the outcome of general elections was heavily tipped in favor of the incumbents, the margin with which the government would win was decided in the open boroughs, and public opinion (at least in the Magyar areas) would at least leave its imprint on the composition of the House of Representatives. Furthermore, in accordance with a tacit parliamentary convention, politically prominent individuals, including the premier, were to run in the open boroughs in order to create the aura of popularity to their regime. Consequently it was not unusual for party leaders to emerge as losers from electoral contests. The "allpowerful" Kálmán Tisza was defeated twice, once in 1878 at the zenith of his career (seeking reelection in the opposition bastion of Debrecen) and then again in 1901, retired from the premiership but still a venerated elder statesman of his party.

These arrangements were no proper substitutes for free and popular elections but they allowed for a degree of flexibility and pluralism in the political process by forcing the professional politicians of the machine to bargain, to provide payoffs and to coopt various interest groups into the ruling Liberal party. In order to control the majority in the House of Representatives any government had to win about 50 seats in addition to the 160 boroughs under bureaucratic patronage. A comfortable margin would require even more extra seats. These would have to come either through buying the support of the wealthy classes or by winning in the open boroughs, or through some combination of the two. The bargaining process woud entail preelection commitments; or else, between elections, raising the prospect of secession from or fusion with the government party. At times these secessions and fusions became so frequent that many observers were inclined to describe them as the functional equivalent of a working two-party system. A detailed description of all these parliamentary maneuvers would require a separate treatment. Here we can only list some of the most massive desertions from the Liberal party: In 1876, sixty-eight deputies defected on account of disagreements with the government's handling of fiscal negotiations with Austria; in 1878, six deputies defected to form an anti-Semitic group under the leadership of Victor Istóczy; in 1894, twenty-eight deputies left the Liberal party on the issue of civil marriage and church-state relations—some of these defectors eventually returning to the fold, others forming their own Catholic People's party; in December 1898, thirty-eight deputies, almost all of them landowning aristocrats, crossed the aisle in protest against Premier Bánffy's handling of appropriations; in 1899, almost the entire conservative opposition fused with the Liberal party only to leave it again in the spring of 1904, whereas in November of the same year two dozen more deputies left to form a new Constitution party on the opposition. During the thirty years of unbroken Liberal rule (1875–1905) the governing party lost, and eventually regained, at least 250 of its parliamentary deputies. The threat of secession always hung over the party, and to avoid them the prime ministers regularly had to consult their entourage. At critical junctures they had to ask for votes of confidence, and the results were often adverse. Kálmán Tisza himself, the architect of machine politics and the founder of the Mameluke Guard, was no exception. At the time of the budget crisis of 1877, for instance, he polled the Liberal caucus: 181 deputies voted for and 69 against his policy while 94 abstained.[16] Two of Tisza's successors (Bánffy in 1899 and Khuen-Héderváry in 1903) were thrown out of their high office by backbench rebellions, the latter by a formal vote of the Liberal rank and file.

   The autocratic tendencies of the system were mitigated and its pluralistic elements further enhanced by a number

---

[16] Gusztáv Gratz, *A dualizmus kora* (The Age of Dualism), (Budapest: Magyar Szemle Társaság, 1934), I, 159.

of habits, conventions, and quasi-institutions that operated as correctives in the absence of free competition and represented built-in restraints on the arbitrary exercise of power. In the last analysis these restraints derived from a long legal and parliamentary tradition shared by the members of the ruling classes. As such, they were most effective in protecting the personal and political rights of the members of the establishment: the gentry and the aristocracy. But at the same time, more by default than by design, they were also instrumental in blunting the harshness of the bureaucratic regime toward the lower classes and the national minorities.

Politically, the most significant of these "correctives" was the practice of parliamentary obstruction. Just as in the leisurely days of the old, feudal Diet, the parliamentary rules of procedure were lax. No restrictions existed about the time allotted to the individual speakers, and such devices as the "kangaroo" or the "guillotine" used in the British Commons and other parliaments to curb debate were unknown. One deputy could challenge the accuracy of the minutes, and only twenty signatures were needed to ask for a roll call. These liberal rules of procedure naturally invited filibustering tactics, in particular so because the opposition parties justly felt that they had little chance to overthrow the government at the polls. When the minority was confronted with a bill that it regarded as deleterious to its vital interests, it either resorted to the holding of marathonic speeches or else to the tactic of "technical obstruction," that is, to innumerable challenges of the minutes and requests for roll calls on petty matters of procedure. In one famous instance, the House of Representatives in a midnight vote decided that the debate should have ended at noon; on another occasion the record of the previous session was challenged twenty-one times, and each challenge rejected by a roll-call vote. Parliamentary obstruction prevented not only the passage of regular bills, but on occasion even routine measures and appropriations. To avoid such embarrassment the prime ministers were forced to bargain with the opposition. Premier Széll, for instance, concluded a regular pact with the opposition upon becoming the head of the government. In it the opposition agreed not to obstruct the election of a new speaker of the House of Representatives and the passage of four bills including appropriations. In exchange the prime minister guaranteed the "cleanness" of the forthcoming elections—that is, no interference with voting in the open boroughs—and pledged to submit legislation to the House to extend the jurisdiction of the High Court of Justice over electoral complaints.[17]

A second significant corrective was provided by the judiciary system acting as the guardian of civil and political rights. Trial by one's own peers had been part of the judicial tradition of the country, at least as far as the nobility was concerned. In 1848 the judicial system was modernized and the old Lord's Bench (*úriszék*)—a court elected by and from the local nobility—was substituted by regular juries (*esküdtszék*) drawn from the voting registers. In disputes that involved citizens and the state these juries tended to be kindly disposed toward their peers and gave the broadest possible interpretation to constitutional law. "In political and libel cases," writes a socialist critic of the old regime, "acquittal was very frequent." [18] The disposition of higher courts was no less lenient. In 1912 the High Court of Justice reversed the sentence of Gyula Kovács, a deputy who fired five shots at István Tisza (Kálmán's son and successor in the chair of the prime minister), on the ground that the assail-

---

17 *Ibid.*, I, 397.
18 Zoltán Horváth, *Magyar Századforduló* (The Turn of the Century in Hungary), (Budapest: Kossuth Kiadó, 1961), p. 337.

ant had acted in the defense of the constitution. Another celebrated case was the libel suit brought by Premier Lukács against Deputy Zoltán Désy who had publicly described the head of the government as the greatest swindler in Europe, accusing him of the misappropriation of public funds. By acquitting Désy, the High Court tacitly acknowledged the validity of the charges and brought about the resignation of the premier. Pursuant to legislation in 1899 the High Court also offered a measure of protection against electoral abuse, at least in the Magyar-inhabited "open" boroughs. In 1901 the court investigated four, in 1905 five, in 1906 four, in 1910 fifty-two complaints.[19] In sixteen of these cases the court ruled for new elections. In these cases the court usually found that the voters of the opposition parties, usually Magyar nationalists or conservatives, had been prevented from reaching the polling place, or otherwise grossly mistreated by the gendarmerie or local administration. When and where the regular courts failed to intercede on behalf of some members of the establishment, the traditional code of honor of the ruling class was invoked to protect its members from the machinations of the government or the bureaucracy. Thus in 1878 a court of honor blackballed Kálmán Tisza for "unparliamentary behavior." Premier Bánffy, although a member of a baronial family, was declared by his fellow aristocrats as "socially unacceptable, a nongentleman, and a person not to be admitted to any social club." While the great Tisza had survived politically the blackballing, Bánffy did not. Other premiers fared better, but many of them had to fight duels and were involved in endless affairs of honor on account of their public activities.

The courts of law were far less favorably disposed to-

---

[19] Reports of the Committee on Credentials. To be found in first and second sessions of the respective volumes of the *Napló*.

ward the rights of the national minorities and of the political representatives of the lower classes. The same juries that indignantly defended the freedom of their peers found no fault in convicting Rumanians and Slovaks for incitement or in sending to jail Socialist agitators. The same High Court that reversed electoral results in Magyar constituencies failed to review complaints by candidates of parties representing the national minorities who claimed that voting registers had been falsified or that votes had been invalidated on rather tenuous grounds. Nor was the court sympathetic to the Agrarian Socialist leader András Achim whose mandate it suspended on the flimsy pretext that his election had been obtained by seditious means. Nevertheless the fact that "political" and libel cases were tried in public, by courts of law and in observance of procedural standards, ensured a measure of fairness and leniency in treatment. Reading about the political trials of the period involving the national minorities and the Socialists one is first struck by the great number of cases in court, then by the relative leniency of the sentences. According to the careful documentation of Robert Seton-Watson, in one critical decade (1898–1908), 503 Slovaks were indicted on charges ranging from incitement to riot to abusing the Hungarian flag, and in 81 trials drew a total of 79 years and 6 months. During the same period 216 Rumanians were sentenced to 38 years and 9 months.[20] These aggregate figures were impressive but a division of years by sentences yields averages of 1.6 and 2.2 months. In most cases the terms were to be served in the nominal captivity of "state confinement" (*ál-lamfogház*). Longer sentences were usually reduced or suspended by executive clemency. In one of the best-known

[20] Robert Seton-Watson, *Racial Problems in Hungary* (London: Constable, 1908), pp. 448–466.

trials of the age, the sixteen authors of the Rumanian Memorandum to the crown were sentenced to a total of 29 years in May 1894. The sentences were appealed and upheld in the higher courts, but on September 17, 1895, all defendants were released from confinement.[21] The records of the Socialist movement, as published by one of its leading members, show 916 indictments in the prewar period resulting in an aggregate sentence of 24 years and 11 months, or an approximate average of 12 days.[22] These repressive measures embittered relations between government and population and on the whole remained ineffective. They could not stem the tide of social and national protest, nor could they serve as a major policy instrument in the hands of the governments in shaping society according to their will. Tradition and the pluralism restrained the coerciveness and in the final analysis restricted the choices open for public policy.

The influx of the gentry had an obvious impact on the character of the bureaucracy and the political machine. Public administration, the ministries, and the "government party" (the perennial Liberal majority) came to resemble huge fraternities of social equals and traditional communities sustained by family relationships and common social symbols rather than the impersonal norms of modern associations. This was evident in various conversational forms. All members of the party and the bureaucracy were expected to use the cordial and familial *te* (corresponding to the German *du*) and it was customary for senior officials to address their subordinates affectionately as "son" (*fiam*) or "younger brother" (*öcsém*) while the latter would address

[21] See *Budapesti Hírlap*, news items on September 18 and 20, 1895.
[22] Vilmos Böhm, *Két forradalom tüzében* (In the Crossfire of Two Revolutions), (Wien: Bécsi Magyar Kiadó, 1923), p. 19.

their superiors as "uncle" (*bátyám*). The use of "Mister" and the third person singular, *maga*, was slightly derogatory and was mainly reserved for outsiders. With the stubbornness of déclassés the gentry bureaucrat also insisted on the external symbols of status and class solidarity. While working as a small clerk or administrative assistant (*fogalmazó*) he might proudly wear the high boots or feathered country hat of his landed cousins or ancestors. Almost ritually he would attend shooting parties and entertain lavishly even though he might have to go hungry for a month afterward. More than ever before, the gentry looked down upon manual labor and shunned economic achievement, an attitude that was most pungently expressed in the gentlemanly *bon mot* that "money was a gift of God to be spent for pleasure." In action this machine was neither conspicuously corrupt nor grossly inept, but the efficient handling of official business was reserved for fellow members of the establishment, while the rest of the public, above all the peasantry, was treated with indifference or outright contempt. If the Balkan idea of service in exchange for petty cash was alien to the system, so was the Anglo-Saxon idea of civil service. By every token, officialdom regarded itself as the master and not the servant of the underlying society.

Yet while carrying forth these traditional symbols and attitudes the gentry of the bureaucracy and the political machine developed an identity of their own as a political class with vested interests in national power and unity. These vested interests took precedence over the particular interests of economic classes. The machine politician now expected that "society succumb to the grandiose demands of state authority." [23] This etatism combined with an ostentatious

---

[23] István Tisza, *Magyar Agrárpolitika* (Hungarian Agrarian Policy), (Budapest: Athaeneum, 1897), p. 18.

anticlericalism—reflecting bureaucratic suspicions of the established church as a major competitor for the loyalties of the citizenry—and a commitment to economic progress and modernization that set the bureaucratic gentry apart from the landed classes. In the name of "progress" the machine politicians of the Liberal party called upon the owners of large and medium estates to adopt efficient modes of production or else abandon their ancestral lands and seek compensation in politics or in the service of the state. In the years following the Compromise the political class came to subscribe to the modern idea that land was a commodity that should go to the highest bidder and the most efficient cultivator: an open invitation to urban capital to take over the ancestral estates of the nobility and to modernize agricultural economy.

Traditional values and contempt for enterpreneurship did not preempt a rational view of economics, but they induced a particular concept of development, so to say, by proxy. The essence of this view was that the declining nobility should perform political rather than economic functions, but at the same time should use the power of the state to protect the business class in its pursuit of wealth. The gentry and their party, the Liberals, aimed at creating what W. W. Rostow calls the "preconditions of a takeoff,"[24] by making the country hospitable to enterpreneurship and capital investment. Accordingly, in the years following the Compromise, the Liberal party sponsored a vast legislative framework in parliament to modernize the legal structure of the country and designed an extensive and costly program to improve the system of public transportation. In the eighties and nineties earlier slogans of economic liberalism

---

[24] Walt. W. Rostow, *The Stages of Economic Growth* (Cambridge, England: The University Press, 1962), pp. 17–35.

were abondoned and the Liberal party became the chief advocate of a policy of subsidies and tax exemptions to encourage industrial growth, without actively engaging the state in processes of production and investment. The major role that the state played in economics was through the artificial depression of wage levels and through shifting the costs of social overhead onto the lower classes to allow higher profits for large enterprise and the competitiveness of Hungarian goods on the Austrian and the Balkan markets.

Though agrarian by social background, the bureaucracy and the professional politicians of the government party leaned toward banking and industrial interests on grounds of long-range political considerations. These "mercantilistic" sympathies (as they were referred to in common parlance) were much evident in party programs and parliamentary legislation—four major and hundreds of minor industrial acts were passed between 1881 and 1913—as well as in budgetary allocations that consistently favored the ministries of industry and commerce over agriculture.[25] In this connection one must also note the extensive ties between finance capital and the parliamentary Liberal party. According to a deposition made by István Rakovsky to the House of Representatives in 1896, fifty-five members of the Liberal party held 77 jobs with railroad and transportation companies while another eighty-six held 93 positions with banks and industrial corporations either as legal advisors or as members of the board.[26] While on numerous occasions the nature of the parliamentary system made them succumb to heavy agrarian pressure, these Liberal deputies and the

---

[25] See Alexander Matlekovits (ed.), *Das Königreich Ungarn statistisch und wirtschaftlich dargestellt* (Leipzig: Duncker und Humblot, 1900), II, 911. From here on quoted as *Das Königreich Ungarn*.

[26] Napló (1896), XXI, 305.

mercantilistic sympathies of the party shielded industry and bank capital from the vengeance of the conservative and agrarian landed aristocracy. In 1898 the yearbook of the Budapest Chamber of Commerce, an organization not taken to an overly optimistic view of business opportunities in the country, could still state that "the wisdom of the parliamentary majority . . . saved the country from the agrarian reaction that has gained ground in Germany and in the Austrian half of the Monarchy."[27]

Bureaucratic perspectives of power, stability and development made the political class the pragmatic defenders of dualism and the Compromise. No less ardently patriotic than their opponents who often denounced them for subservience, they upheld the settlement not as an act of loyalty to the dynasty but as an instrument of furthering Hungarian interests inside and outside the country. They would argue with good reason that the partnership with Austria, although falling short of contemporary models of the national state, had tangible economic advantages and in addition gave Hungary a disproportionate influence in European politics. The protagonists of this view could always point to Andrássy's tenure of office as the foreign minister of the monarchy and his success in promoting policies inspired by Magyar fears of panslavism and Russian domination. Indeed, an independent Hungary with sixteen or eighteen million inhabitants (half of them hostile national minorities) could hardly have hoped to make similar excursions into great power diplomacy. Moreover, the Hungarian ruling circles had a dynamic view of the dual arrangement in that they entertained the hope that one day

---

[27] *A budapesti kereskedelmi és iparkamara évkönyve* (Yearbook of the Chamber of Commerce and Industry of Budapest), (Budapest: Pesti könyvwyomda, 1899), pp. 15–16.

the center of power would shift from Vienna to Budapest. In the meantime the Liberal governments of Hungary jealously guarded their constitutional autonomy and pre- rogatives. The slightest hint of Austrian intervention into domestic politics was met by immediate rebuttal. Thus when the Austrian premier Kroeber once ventured an opin- ion on Hungarian constitutional law, his counterpart in Budapest dismissed the speech as the *dilettante* view of a "distinguished foreigner." The Hungarian governments al- so doggedly resisted Austrian attempts to modify the quotas of common expenditures established by the Compromise. Between 1867 and 1890 the Hungarian quota increased by a mere 1.5 per cent despite considerable increases in the sources of public revenue. In 1897 an irate Austrian delega- tion demanded a new 42 to 58 division of expenditures but Hungarian obduracy forced them to settle at 32.5 to 67.5.[28] The bargaining methods of the Hungarian governments were reckless and reflected the low political integration of the Austro-Hungarian monarchy. Far from being satisfied with the role of a subservient junior partner, the Hungarian political class tried to make the best out of the dualist ar- rangement, bickering for new advantages at every turn.

The political machine and the Liberal party of Kálmán Tisza were closely identified with the gentry, yet not all the gentry were absorbed by the state and the bureaucracy. While perhaps 40 to 50,000 of them became civil servants in the two decades following the Compromise, an equal or even larger number remained outside with no access to the "pork barrel" that the machine could provide. A percentage of this "unabsorbed" gentry were educated mostly in the legal profession. Others were on the way to complete social

---

[28] Arthur May, *The Hapsburg Monarchy, 1867–1914* (Cambridge, Mass.: Harvard University Press, 1960), pp. 348–349.

ruin. They were forced to enter low-class pursuits and survived only as a frustrated noble proletariat. These underprivileged groups on the whole shared the socio-economic and political perspectives of the incumbent Liberal party. But as their hopes faded to find status and security in the bureaucracy, they turned into a bitter political opposition that saw Hungary's salvation (as well as their own) not in the continued partnership with Austria, but in the expansion of the national state so that its institutions could accommodate the declining gentry class in its entirety.

This socially threatened and economically deprived element served as the backbone and chief supporter of the Party of Eighteen Forty-eight (in deference to the revolution of that year). Founded in 1868, this party first attracted only a miniscule fraction of the electorate, but as economic conditions deteriorated in the eighties and nineties, the Forty-eighters gained ground in parliament where they loudly denounced the concept of common affairs as "mock constitutionalism" and a figleaf for foreign domination. In their programs they advocated the dissolution of the customs union as the precondition of economic growth and clamored for an independent Hungarian army. This last point was of particular and immediate importance to the supporters of the party not only as an instrument of national power but also as an attractive refuge for the declining gentry permitting the rise of a genuine Hungarian Junker class in the place of the despised imperial corps of officers with its alien language and spirit.

In its official declarations the party stopped short of advocating the dissolution of the dual monarchy, but unofficially its members left little doubt that this indeed was their ultimate objective. In the place of the monarchy the Forty-eighters envisaged the rise of a "greater Hungary," spinning a web of imperialistic fantasies that the destitute gentry was willing to take for political reality. According to a number of writers close to the nationalist opposition Hungary would gather sufficient strength in the twentieth century to impose her will on the neighboring countries and emerge as a European great power on her own. "Today the Hungarian nation is still in a transitory stage," wrote the nationalist journalist and deputy Pál Hoitsy in 1902. "She is strong enough to resist encroachments coming from the outside, but not yet strong enough to embark upon the road of conquest." [29] However, according to Hoitsy, Hungary would shortly annex Bosnia, Dalmatia, and the other smaller territories that had been her tributaries in the Middle Ages. "She may or may not annex Serbia." In any case, the future generations will live to see Hungarian supremacy over Bulgaria and hear Hungarian spoken on the streets of Sofia."[30] Rumania's fate would be the same, for her people did not possess the true qualities needed to create and sustain an independent state. These territorial conquests would ensure markets for Hungarian industry yet to be developed at a grand scale and no doubt would require large numbers of military and administrative personnel thus providing the unintegrated gentry and would-be bureaucrat with a sense of hope, pride, and purpose.

This intemperate pauper element was not alone in rejecting the provisions of the Compromise. They found allies among the members of the rapidly dwindling squirearchy and the Protestant smallholding class of eastern Hungary who gathered under the banner of the National Independence party founded in 1874. The party was a close ally of the Forty-eighters on the constitutional issue. At a

---

[29] Paul Hoitsy, *Nagymagyarország* (Greater Hungary), (Budapest: Lampel, 1902), p. 7.
[30] *Ibid.*, p. 102.

number of times the two parties even fused under common leadership and the name "National Independence (1848) Party," but each time they split up again into separate parliamentary factions. Of the two parties the Independents represented a more conservative and moderate force who were content to advocate such reforms as the modification of the imperial escutcheon to include the Hungarian coats-of-arms, national colors for Hungarian regiments, and Hungarian consular representation in foreign countries.[31] As to relations with Austria, the Independents insisted on a constructive dialogue and on the revision, rather than the abolition, of the Compromise. "Common affairs are a reality," wrote the Transylvanian deputy Miklós Bartha, "they can be reformed gradually but not abolished overnight. The way to reform them is to win a parliamentary majority and to become the government of His Majesty." [32] Characteristically, the Independent program of 1884 started out with a pledge of loyalty to the Crown, lamenting only the absence of a Hungarian royal court "in which our magnates could feel at home and would not be treated as alien intruders." [33] This last sentence may well have been written by one of the Calvinist peers of Transylvania whose numbers were in fact sparsely represented in the court of Vienna.

In contrast to the nationalist gentry, the *latifundiary* aristocracy, the owners of large estates, was willing to accept the constitutional provisions of the Compromise, but generally felt uneasy about the social and economic policies of the bureaucratic state. Not all big landowners of the period were aristocrats, nor were all aristocrats big landowners, but

---

[31] Gyula Mérei, *Magyar politikai pártprogrammok* (Hungarian Party Programs), (Budapest: Ranschburg, 1934), pp. 121–125.

[32] *Ellenzék* (Kolozsvár), September 23, 1898.

[33] Mérei, *op. cit.*, p. 117.

those who were—the "magnates," to distinguish them from
landless peers or landowners without title—represented the
hard core of traditional conservatism in Hungarian politics. They were a small and exclusive group who in public
as well as in private sought to dissociate themselves from
the liberal fads and symbols of the age and would refer to
themselves with engaging frankness as clericals or reaction-
aries.

To be sure, one would find an ample number of magnates among the members of the Liberal party, a fact that
generally led historians to conclude that no conflict of interest existed between the landed aristocracy and the bureaucratic state machine. What is overlooked here is that
the latifundiary aristocracy had preserved its separate identity irrespective of party label and that the magnates, due
to their economic independence, would be fickle as parliamentary allies. The aristocratic deputies who one day as
members of the Liberal party would support the government on one issue, could turn their back on it on another.
Indeed, leading conservative figures—Counts Albert Apponyi, Pál Széchenyi, Robert Zselénszky, Sándor Károlyi, or
Gyula Andrássy, Jr.—constantly changed their party affiliation, serving at times as members of the Cabinet while at
others as the leaders of various conservative parties of the
parliamentary opposition.

In the history of the period we can observe several
major cycles of conservative-liberal (or bureaucratic-
aristocratic) cooperation and antagonism. Between 1867 and
1875 the aristocracy loyally supported Ferenc Deák, the architect of the Compromise, and his political party. However, in 1875, disgruntled with the government's economic
policy and resentful of gentry predominance in the Liberal
party twenty-six aristocratic politicians seceded and formed
a Conservative party of their own. The life of this party

lasted until 1884 when it faded into a more diluted moderate opposition whose members would oscillate between the two sides of the aisle generally supporting the Liberal party on constitutional issues and exhorting socioeconomic concessions in exchange. The conservative-liberal division hardened again in 1892 when the issue of church-state relations was put before parliament. Then in 1899 an aristocratic maneuver precipitated the fall of Bánffy which in turn led to a new fusion between the liberal "old guard" and the conservatives led by Albert Apponyi. The price exacted by the conservatives was an end to aggressive anticlericalism and a boost in agricultural tariffs, the biggest in the fifty years of the Austro-Hungarian customs union. Yet tensions between the two wings did not abate, and the conservatives pulled out again in 1904 to set up a new Constitution party in alliance with the national radicals of the Independence and Forty-eight parties. This bizarre alliance of dynastic conservatives and national radicals, agrarians and industrializers, won the subsequent elections of 1905 and 1906, but the coalition split up after three years. In 1910 the majority of conservatives joined the National Party of Work, founded by István Tisza to replace the old Liberal party.

Whereas the gentry was willing to accept "progress" for reasons of national power, the aristocrat had strong misgivings about the disruptive consequences of social and economic change. For the magnates modernization implied a direct threat to social status and economic influence, and they responded with attempts to slow down or even halt the process of social transformation. Thus the Conservative Manifesto of 1876, a remarkable document even by the standards of the time, although stopping short of endorsing feudal institutions, took issue with the legal and political reforms of 1848 as detrimental to the stability of social relations. "Now that physical punishment has been abolished," the writer of the conservative program complained, "masters are defenseless against the insolence of their servants." The author then makes the following observation: "Instead of being caned the poor man is now subjected to imprisonment and visited by heavy fines. This practice threatens the physical survival of his family." [34] Throughout the programmatic work there is a transparent anxiety about the loss of aristocratic influence. The writer not only denounces the "finance oligarchy" but also "the pennyless desperadoes of public life," [35] meaning the professional politicians of the gentry class, and espouses the principle that the landed aristocracy alone possesses the innate capacities of responsible political leadership.

By social instinct and economic interest the aristocratic conservatives were agrarians and the mainstay of a vigorous pressure group for higher tariffs on grain, lower taxes, and subsidies to agricultural estates. Their economic principles were succinctly summarized by Sándor Károlyi, the author of the agrarian program of 1902: "What is good for agriculture is good for the country. We must judge all policies by this standard for three-quarters of the population derive their livelihood from agricultural production. If industry serves the purposes of agricultural development it should be subsidized. If it is detrimental to agrarian interests, it should perish." [36] But conservative agrarianism did not merely imply the pragmatic, if overly selfish, pursuit of economic interests. It was rather the cornerstone of a comprehensive social program and political philosophy. The

---

[34] János Asboth, *Magyar Conservativ politika* (Hungarian Conservative Policy), (Budapest, 1876), p. 26.

[35] *Ibid.*, p. 113.

[36] *Napló*, XXI (1895), 230.

conservative agrarian was not content to influence the prices, the market or agricultural legislation. He attacked the foundations of market economy and modern society:

> In the struggle for wealth, the stronger trampled upon the weaker and the less shrewd. Only usurers are benefitting from the misery created by the artificial principle of equality. Unrestricted economic competition is also detrimental to patriotic feeling and is bound to destroy loyalty to king and country. What the agrarians want is the restoration of the ethics of the previous ages, above all in the sphere of production and social relations.[37]

These agrarian interests also contributed to the shaping of the magnates' attitude toward the constitutional problem and the Compromise, for the close relations with the western half of the monarchy and in general the maintenance of the constitutional *status quo* gave access to the secure Austrian and Bohemian markets for Hungarian agriculture. Yet the aristocracy's attachment to the partnership with Austria did not solely rest on pragmatic considerations, for in their case economic interest converged with a long tradition of loyalty to the common dynasty. And since the Crown and the dynasty coexisted uneasily in the framework of dualism, this attachment also implied that the landed aristocracy could never accept the idea of the national state without reservations. Whereas the traditional ruling classes of Germany, Britain, and France eventually submitted to the national idea because they could identify it with the Crown—the main symbol of national unity—the Hun-

---

[37] Sándor Károlyi, "Manifesto of the Agrarians" (also known as "Letter from Göncz"). Quoted in Antal Balla, *A magyar Országgyülés története* (History of the Hungarian Parliament), (Budapest: Légrády, 1927), p. 182.

garian aristocrat felt compelled to make a choice between the two and opted for the latter in preference to the gentry nation and the bureaucratic state. In political theory this implied a juxtaposition of the ideas of a religious and national community with a stress on the primacy and moral superiority of the former. In practical politics this attitude implied an opposition to the aggressive nationalist policies of the Magyar gentry, and a measure of sympathy for the oppressed national minorities. If in fact the aristocracy threw no obstacles in the path of these policies, they rarely used their prestige to promote them actively.

Last but not least the aristocracy and the gentry were split on the issue of domestic political organization. The aristocrats shared the gentry's reservations concerning the extension of political rights to the lower classes, but at the same time they were also opposed to the creeping authoritarianism of the two Tiszas and resented the bureaucratic encroachments upon the local influence of the landowning classes. The conservatives denounced the practices introduced by Kálmán and István Tisza, not from the viewpoint of democracy but of oligarchy, representing a traditional *fronde* against the modern, bureaucratized state apparatus. In politics, as in economics, the conservative magnates advocated a return to the practices of previous ages, that is, to the free-wheeling electoral contests of pre-1848 times. In the Hungary of the late nineteenth century the landowning classes could argue with some justification that tyranny was modern and pluralism was traditional. Therefore it is not surprising to find the representatives of the most reactionary socioeconomic views, like Albert Apponyi or the younger Andrássy, among those who consistently had on their lips pleas for political liberty and for a "government based on covenants, laws and equity." These pleas became particularly vocal around the turn of the century when under the pretext of suppressing agitation among the national minorities Premiers Bánffy and István Tisza attempted to smash some of the electoral strongholds of aristocratic conservatism. In response, the aristocratic *frondeurs* founded the Puros movement consisting of aristocratic deputies from all major parties. The movement was designed to restore "integrity and honesty in public life," and to end the "one-party system, the odious institution of the government party with its predictable majorities that kill courageous and free political discussion."[38] In the nineties this group had considerable, if intermittent, influence on public opinion. They blocked attempts to destroy the last vestiges of municipal autonomy, campaigned for the fairness of electoral practices, sponsored a parliamentary code of ethics, and at the same time used their political weight to maintain a highly restrictive franchise. Like the great Whig dukes of Georgian England they defended the political rights of the landed class against the overbearance of central power but had no sympathy for the idea of popular government.

The gentry, while making politics and administration its business, also set definite patterns of social mobility for the rest of the society. The glitter of gentry life, however false and superficial, had always had great attractions for the middle classes. Now the power and status of the bureaucracy made these attractions almost irresistible. If and when the offspring of a well-to-do horse trader or peasant was exposed to higher education, his ambition was almost invariably to emulate the nobility by joining public administration hoping to reach the apex represented by the machinery of parliamentary politics. What was more remarkable, the members of the preindustrial bourgeoisie, the "sober" Ger-

---

[38] The words of Dezsö Szilágyi, in Gratz, *op. cit.,* I, 211.

man burghers of the northern mining communities, the
Greek traders of Buda and Pest, the Armenian merchants
of Transylvanian cities, all fell in line and by the end of
the century were willing to relinquish economics for politics. The explanation for this remarkable social phenomenon must be tentative, but most likely had something to do
with the prolonged stagnation of the traditional urban economy, the high risks of entrepreneurship, and the chronic
shortages of capital in Hungarian society. From 1880 on
these groups show an increased educational mobility and
formed one of the potential new sources of bureaucratic recruitment.

The aversion of the gentry from economic pursuits and
the demoralization of the old commercial bourgoisie created a vacuum that was rapidly filled in by the Jewish population of the country. In 1842 Hungary had a Jewish population of about one quarter of a million subjected to various
occupational and residential restrictions. The reforms of
1848-1849 removed these handicaps, and the Jewish inhabitants of the country began to move toward the cities and
the rising modern sector of the economy. At the same time
massive Jewish immigration started from outside the country. Augmented by this influx, the original (1842) number
of Jews doubled by 1868 and almost quadrupled by 1910.
Their percentage of the total population increased from
2.4 to 5.1.[39] The bulk of the immigrants came from the
east, from Galicia, Russia, and Rumania, while from the
west came a much smaller number—mostly established businessmen and financiers with personal connections to the
banks of Austria, Germany, and France.

---

[39] Based on official census figures as they appear in Péter Újváry (ed.)
Magyar zsidó lexikon (Hungarian Jewish Encyclopedia), (Budapest:
Pallas, 1929), p. 553. From here on quoted as *Magyar zsidó lexikon*.

Unencumbered by traditional status aspirations and by the irrational features of the Hungarian *Herrenideal* these newcomers took up the task of modernizing Hungary's backward economy with admirable skill and success. In a matter of less than one generation they created the foundations of modern banking, commerce, and industry, contributing at the same time a great deal to the rise of a modern, urban civilization. In the process, more than elsewhere in post-traditional Europe, they became identified with entrepreneurship. The bourgeoisie became largely Jewish, and the Jewish community came close to represent the bourgeoisie. No official statistics correlating religion and occupation exist for the period, but those taken shortly after the end of World War I (for the diminished territory of Hungary) may give us some idea concerning the economic and occupational structure of the Jewish community. According to the census of 1920, 39.7 per cent of the Jewish population was dependent on commerce and banking, 34.3 per cent on industry and mining, 8.7 per cent on the professions, 3.5 per cent were active in transport, and 5.1 per cent were rentiers. Conversely, 53 per cent of all who engaged in commerce (66.2 per cent in Budapest), 80 per cent of the population active in finance (90.3 in the capital), and 12.7 per cent of all self-employed in industry (including handicraft) were of the Jewish faith.[40] In all these occupational categories Jews tended to occupy the middle and higher brackets of the economic scale. In the same census 24.2 per cent of gainfully employed Jewish persons are shown in menial and working-class occupations as opposed to 65.9 per cent in the profes-

---

[40] Magyar Királyi Statisztikai Hivatal, *Recensement de la Population en 1920* (Budapest, 1926). Some of the compiled figures quoted from C. A. Macartney, *October Fifteenth: A History of Modern Hungary, 1929–1945* (Edinburgh: The University Press, 1961), I, 19.

sions, salaried employment, and small entrepreneurship, and 9.9 per cent in the big entrepreneurial and managerial category (employing 20 or more workers). At the apex of the social scale one would find a dozen or so families, the interrelated Kohner, Ullman, Herzog, Deutsch, Weiss, Mauthner, Madarassy-Beck, Lánczy, Chorin, and Goldberger clans, who among themselves controlled the largest Hungarian holding banks and through them nine-tenths of the country's heavy industries. Though the postwar estimates of 24 and 28.8 per cent [41] for the Jewish share in national income may be exaggerated, their control in property and wealth made them the most affluent 5 per cent of the population.

The immigration and embourgeoisement of the Jewish population was welcome and encouraged by official Hungary. The bureaucratic state reached out its arms to the bourgeoisie and was ready to protect it not only as an entrepreneurial class but also as a religious minority. At a time when pogroms raged in Russia and Rumania, and when even in neighboring Austria an irritating anti-Semitism was increasingly accepted as part of political life, in Hungary Jews were extolled by the prime minister as an "industrious and constructive segment of the population" while anti-Semitism was denounced as "shameful, barbarous and injurious to the national honor." [42] The Liberal party was an enthusiastic champion of Jewish emancipation, and waged a long campaign to incorporate Jews as full members of the national community. This campaign culminated in the great legislative battles of 1892–1895 as a result of which the Jewish communities were granted the same

---

[41] See Lázló Levatich, "Nemzeti Jövedelem és jövedelemlosztás" (National Income and Income Distribution), *Budapesti Hírlap*, January 25, 1935.

[42] Kálmán Tisza, *Napló* (1882), V, 64–65.

privileges as the Catholic and Protestant churches, and their representatives were seated in the House of Lords. By contemporaries as well as posterity the "Jewish question" was regarded as the touchstone of liberalism, so much so that at a later date the words "liberal" and "philo-Semitic" were often used as synonyms in Hungarian common parlance.

By the other side the patronage and protection of official Hungary was paid back with interest. The immigrants adopted their new country with spontaneity and enthusiasm, and within a generation became Magyar in language and identity. In 1880, 58.5 per cent of all Jews gave Magyar as their mother tongue, in 1910, 77.8 per cent.[43] This newly assimilated element "was often more loyalist than Apponyi, more chauvinistic than Ugron; they composed Magyar songs, wrote romantic poems, and when they founded new factories they did so 'for the benefit of the fatherland.' "[44] In the provinces inhabited by the national minorities the bourgeoisie became an outpost of Magyar culture. In the Rumanian and Slovak villages Jewish shopkeepers or country doctors were often the only persons to speak the Magyar tongue among the inhabitants, hence they tended to become the natural allies of the local bureaucracy, the notary and the chief of the gendarmes representing the government of Budapest. As a Jewish member of parliament stated in 1895:

> Statistics prove that the Jews of the districts inhabited by nationalities carry on a regular missionary work. Statistics also prove that for miles around not a Magyar word is to be heard—in Rumanian, Slovak or German districts—it is a Jewish family living in the most modest circumstances which not only cultivates the Magyar language in its own

---

[43] *Hungarian Peace Negotiations*, I, 107.
[44] Horváth, *op. cit.*, p. 56. Apponyi was one of the leaders of the Conservatives, Ugron a leader of the Independence party.

circle, but also does its best to inoculate its children with
the Magyar language and culture. We see that he who in
the non-Magyar districts wishes his children to learn the
Magyar language sends them to the Jewish school.[45]

In politics, banking and industrial oligarchs provided financial support for the Tisza machine while the petite bourgeoisie dutifully cast its ballots for the candidates of the
government party. Budapest where one of every four inhabitants and one of every two voters was Jewish, Liberal
deputies were elected with impressive majorities. These
acts of loyalty earned the lavish praise of official Hungary
and prompted some Austrians to quip derisively about
"Judeo-Magyardom" and the city of "Judapest."

Common interests and political cooperation notwithstanding, for decades the Jewish bourgeoisie remained
somewhat isolated from the mainstream of Hungarian life,
though the causes of this were more social than racial or
religious. Nineteenth-century society erected walls of separation around social classes, and there was no more social
intercourse between gentry and aristocracy than between
bureaucracy and bourgeoisie. Most symbolic of this social
separation was the existence of three prominent and powerful clubs in Budapest. The oldest and most distinguished of
the three, the National Casino, was the gathering place of
the aristocracy; the Countrywide Club (*Országos*) was pat-
ronized by the gentry and the professional politicians, while
the wealthy bourgeoisie congregated in the Leopold District
Casino (*Lipótvárosi*) in the heart of the financial quarter of
Budapest. The barriers of class were never transgressed in
these clubs. The National Casino did not accept the gentry,
and the Countrywide Club would have nothing to do with
businessmen. In general, social exchanges among the three

---

[45] Quoted in Seton-Watson, op. cit., p. 188.

classes were rare and highly formalized. Whereas the informal address was compulsory among the members of the gentry and politicians, the same address was almost never used between the gentry and the aristocracy or with members of the bourgeoisie. If invitations were issued across caste lines the ladies were usually excluded to emphasize the business-like character of the occasion. The annual balls of the aristocracy, the gentry, and the business community had separate guest lists. If in the capital social relations among these three groups were scant, in the countryside they were absolutely nonexistent.[46]

On the turn of the century this rigid caste system began to melt away and the bourgeoisie began to gain recognition through its wealth. In the first decade of the new century no less than twenty-six Jewish families were raised to baronial rank, and another two-hundred and eighty were granted titles of common nobility.[47] The number of conversions increased, and intermarriage was common after 1896.[48] In this respect the upper classes led the way and, as an anti-Semitic writer of a later period would ruefully note, at least sixteen scions of prominent aristocratic clans took bribes from prosperous Jewish families to gild their ancestral escutcheons with commercial wealth.[49] Anti-Semitism was at its lowest ebb and the bourgeoisie was on its way to social ascendancy. Yet almost simultaneously the second and third

---

[46] For the social relations of the period see, among others, Miklós Zay, "A zsidók a társadalomban" (Jews in Society), *Huszadik Század*, VIII (1908), 948; Horváth, *op. cit.*, p. 34; Zoltán Lippay, *op. cit.*, p. 31 ff.

[47] Klaus Schickert, *Die Judenfrage in Ungarn* (Essen: Essener Verlagsanstalt, 1943), p. 128.

[48] 393 per annum in the years 1896–1900, 844 per annum in 1911–1915. See Alajos Kovács, *A zsidóság térfoglalása Magyarországon* (The Ascendancy of the Jews in Hungary), (Budapest: Kellner, 1922), p. 26.

[49] Schickert, *op. cit.*, p. 141.

generations of Jewish immigrants, assimilated in language
and culture, began to shy away from economic occupations
and move toward the professions and the bureaucracy in
competition with the native element. It was in this context
that the issues of race and religion assumed some special
significance for gentry society, though latent suspicions and
antagonism did not burst into the open until and after the
revolutions of 1918–1919.

Meanwhile, propelled by government support, foreign
capital, and the entrepreneurial skills of the new bourgeoisie, the economy of the country underwent significant
transformations. In the years between 1867 and 1890 com-
mercialization and market economy made significant advances, and in the nineties, after a long delay, the industrialization of the country began. The population of urban
centers, and in particular of Budapest, rapidly increased.
From 1880 to 1910 the agricultural population declined
from 87 to 62.4 per cent, and the number of those dependent
on industry increased from 6.7 to 18.2 per cent.[50] The railroad network expanded spectacularly from 1945 km in 1865
to 16,888 km at the turn of the century to become one of the
densest in Europe.[51]

These changes had a profound impact on the political
profile of Hungarian society by creating a wider public and
by increasing the political consciousness of the lower classes,
particularly of the urban proletariat. The latter began to
assert itself first in the sixties and seventies by forming
various workman's associations, but the movement gained
momentum only with the rise of a class of factory laborers

---

[50] Dezsö Pap, *A magyar szociálpolitika a világháborúban* (Hungarian
Social Policy in the World War), (Budapest: Grill, 1934), p. xlvi.
[51] *Hungarian Peace Negotiations*, IV, 4.

employed in the large industrial compounds of the capital
(Table II).

Table II. THE DISTRIBUTION OF THE INDUSTRIAL LABOR FORCE,
1900 AND 1910

| | 1900 | | 1910 | |
	Number	*Percent*	*Number*	*Percent*
Independent craftsmen	301,026	33.7	330,975	29.5
Workers of Small enterprises (1–20)	361,665	40.5	375,166	33.4
Factory workers (20+)	230,641	25.8	416,543	37.1
TOTAL	893,332	100.0	1,222,684	100.0

SOURCE: Dezsö Pap, *A magyar szociálpolitika a világháborúban*
(Hungarian Social Policy in the World War), (Budapest: Grill, 1934),
p. xlvi.

Thus is was not until about 1890 that effective working-class
organizations made their appearance, but after that date
both trade unions and the Socialist party rapidly gained in
strength. In 1897–1898 Socialist unions led illegal but successful strike movements in Budapest. In 1901 the Social
Democratic party put up 58 candidates for the general elections, none of whom was returned to parliament under the
highly restrictive franchise. Yet without parliamentary representation, the urban working class became a force to be
reckoned with. At the turn of the century the Social Democratic party had 72,000 members while the affiliated unions
enlisted 107,000 workers, 55.2 per cent of them in Budapest.[52] This membership was the largest any organization
ever had in Hungary. Moreover, this was a militant cadre
with the help of which the Socialists could easily mobilize
150,000–200,000 workers for street demonstrations and soli-

[52] *Das Königreich Ungarn*, II, 354; Pap, op. cit., p. 32.

darity strikes. This they did regularly between 1906 and 1913, when on at least a dozen occasions they shut down public utilities and means of public transportation and turned the streets of Budapest into a bloody battleground between themselves and the police. "Before the mid-nineties," the conservative historian of the period notes, "it was the university youth who organized the demonstrations at times of great political excitement. However in and after 1896 the Social Democrats monopolized the streets. . . . They, and only they could call out the Masses."[53]

The governments of the day first regarded the politicization of the working class as an aberration and responded with a string of coercive measures. "Are you industrial workers?" the minister of the interior addressed a delegation in 1875. "Then you should work industriously. You do not have to bother with anything else. You do not need associations and if you mix in politics, I will teach you a lesson that you never forget."[54] Subsequently the workers' associations were harassed, their leaders arrested and hauled into courts, and their members placed under police surveillance. Riots were put down by gendarmes and soldiers firing into crowds or charging them with fixed bayonets. Repression reached its peak under Bánffy's premiership (1895–1899) when, a recently published source claims, 51 workers were killed and 114 wounded in pitched battles with law-enforcement authorities.[55]

At the same time, however, there was also a gradual realization that working-class radicalism was not an ephemeral phenomenon and that the proletariat would have to

[53] Gratz, op. cit., Vol. I, 351.

[54] Julius Bunzel, Studien zur Sozial und Wirtschaftspolitik Ungarns, (Leipzig: Duncker und Humblot, 1902), p. 94.

[55] Erik Molnár (ed.), Magyarország története (The History of Hungary, (Budapest: Gondolat), II, 149.

be placated by material and social benefits. The major advocate of this policy was the younger Tizsa who, like many other liberals, regarded the rise of the working class as a necessary evil and as a price to be paid for economic progress. "The problem of the workers," he stated in 1891, "was not created here in parliament, but by the growth of manufacturing industries in our country. The rise of the working class is an inevitable concomitant of industrialization and a problem common to all modern societies." [56] Though Tisza in a truly Marxist fashion believed that there were irreconcilable contradictions between labor and capital, he also thought that "a class raised to decent human standards would be less dangerous than a morally and materially deprived mass of humanity that has nothing to lose." [57] In this spirit parliament enacted a series of measures between 1893 and 1897 to improve the condition of industrial workers, including laws providing for extensive medical and accident insurance benefits designed to cover two-thirds of Hungary's labor force in the manufacturing industries, construction, mining, and public transportation. These acts were dictated by purely political considerations as can be seen from the fact that they excluded the less volatile working force of handicraft industries and small enterprise.[58]

Even more significant were the measures that permitted workers to bargain for higher wages. István Tisza first advocated the freedom of collective bargaining in 1897,[59] and under his premiership he restored the right to strike, outlawed by the Penal Code of 1878.[60] This measure was

---

[56] *Napló* (1891), XXII, 45.
[57] *Ibid.*
[58] Bunzel, *op. cit.*, pp. 138–144.
[59] *Napló* (1897), III, 258–265.
[60] Ministry of the Interior, No. 55–154–1904.

portentous in that it represented a modification of earlier policies of the Liberal party that had given unconditional support to capital. Now under the threat of social rebellion the Liberals inaugurated a policy of "paying off" workers at the expense of the bourgeoisie, while still curtailing their participation in politics. As a result, money wages increased substantially, between 1901–1913, though some of the gains were eventually cancelled out by steep increases in the cost of living that were common to all European countries in the decade preceding World War I.[61]

The industrial working class, however, represented less than one-tenth of the labor force and the large majority of the population was still dependent on agriculture. A small part of this agricultural population was peasant smallholders, while a more substantial number was landless. In between the two there was a stratum of subsistence farmers who produced food for their own consumption and had to supplement their income by wage labor at large and medium-size estates. All in all, in 1895, 47.7 per cent of all land was held by .7 per cent of all agricultural proprietors in parcels of 100 yokes (141 acres) or larger and only the rest were shared by the millions of peasant cultivators.[62] The latter included some 36,000 prosperous farmers (the owners of 50–100 yokes), 1.2 million smallholders (5–50 yokes), and 1.27 million "dwarf holders" who owned less than 5 yokes of land. Some 2 million heads of families, or 33.8 per cent of the agricultural and 24.5 per cent of the total labor force,[63] owned no land at all and represented the lowest economic stratum in society. More than anything else it was

[61] See, for instance, A. R. Prest, *Consumers' Experience in the United Kingdom, 1900–1918* (Cambridge, England: The University Press, 1954), pp. 5–10.

[62] Mihály Kerék, *A magyar földkérdés* (The Land Question in Hungary, (Budapest: Egyetemi Nyomda, 1939), p. 63.

[63] Bunzel, *op. cit.*, p. 2.

this impoverished mass that was responsible for the sullen and demoralized quality of Hungarian rural life even in comparison to countries like Bulgaria and Serbia where *per capita* agricultural income and production were far lower.

The agricultural proletariat was not only excluded from the benefits of property ownership but, through a highly inequitable system of taxation, it had to contribute a disproportionate share to public expenditures, and indirectly it had to pay for much of the costs of agricultural growth. From the 1860's on it was one of the cardinal principles of Hungarian economic policy, first enunciated by the Viennese professor Bontoux,[64] that the only way to accumulate domestic capital in the country was through the artificial depression of wage levels in the agricultural sector. This the governments accomplished by a variety of devices, the gendarme's bayonet being the most simple and common of all. After 1884 money wages improved but now the agricultural laborers, through the rising price of staples, had to absorb some of the costs of tariff protectionism. Finally, in the last decade of the nineteenth century the rural proletariat began to feel the consequences of the gradual mechanization of production. According to one estimate, for the average laborer the harvesting season declined from 60 to 24 days, the total number of working days from 200 to 150.[65] In short, while nominal wages increased the standard of living stagnated and eventually declined by an estimated 10 to 20 percent over the last twenty-five years of the nineteenth century.[66]

---

[64] Eugen Bontoux, *Ungarn und die Ernährung Europas* (Wien: Waldheim, 1868).

[65] See Ferenc Eckhardt, *A magyar közgazdaság száz éve* (One-Hundred Years of Hungarian Economy), (Budapest: Posner, 1943), p. 113; Bunzel, *op. cit.*, p. 5.

[66] Kornél Bernátsky, *"Rural Standard of Living in Hungary"* (mimeographed), (New York: Mid-European Studies Center, 1954), pp. 1-2.

These oppressive conditions notwithstanding the Hungarian countryside was quiet and seemingly complacent for almost twenty-five years after the Compromise. In 1890 an aristocratic deputy in the House of Representatives could still favorably compare the peasant with the urban proletariat and extol his traditional virtues: "He does not organize meetings. He does not chant the International. He works if he has a job. If he does not have a job he goes out to find one. And if he can't find one he goes without eating and does not complain. No one in this country is more honest and patient than the farm laborer."[67] But this calm was deceptive. While on the surface nothing seems to have changed, underneath there had been a substantial erosion of traditional values and social perspectives. Between 1867 and 1890 literacy had spread, the railroad network expanded and the volume of social communications had rapidly increased (Table III). The peasants had developed a new

Table III. SOME INDICES OF SOCIAL MOBILIZATION, 1870–1900

	(percent) Literacy	Volume of (thousands) first-class mail	(km) Railroads
1870	34.4	32.5	2,736
1880	40.3	79.6	7,058
1890	45.4	171.9	10,870
1900	51.8	280.0 (1897)	16,928

SOURCES: *Das Königreich Ungarn*, II, 585 and 764. *Hungarian Peace Negotiations*, IV, 4.

awareness of the world and of themselves, and their simmering frustrations were soon to burst into the open. In 1891 there were bloody riots in the county of Békés with large crowds besieging the seat of the local administration. In the next few years the situation in the countryside de-

---

[67] Baron Andreánszki; *Napló* (1890), XVI, 183.

teriorated. In some parts of the country, Bunzel reports, it was not safe for landowners to walk around even in broad daylight.[68] In 1894 one of the peasant leaders, J. Szántó-Kovács, was arrested and his trial in the district court of Hódmezövásárhely triggered another wave of violence that resulted in the imposition of martial law. In 1896–1897 ill-organized agrarian unions struck the grain harvest and fought pitched battles against imported strike breakers and military units brought in for their protection. Notoriously hard to organize, the agricultural proletariat could not sustain their revolutionary momentum in the face of the overwhelming armed strength of the authorities, but a few years later succeeded where the industrial workers had failed: they could send two of their representatives Vilmos Mezöffi and András Achim to the lower house.

For students of political sociology, the agricultural movements of Hungary should be particularly interesting because they were concentrated not in the most impoverished but in the most prosperous areas of the country, in the triangle between the rivers Tisza and Maros that subsequently acquired the name Stormy Corner (*Viharsarok*). It was here in the rich black-belt of the Hungarian Plain that the great riots and harvest strikes occurred. In an apparent parodox the incidence of rural violence was highest in the counties where the best wages were being paid and where the distribution of land was the most equitable. Whereas wages in the northern highlands ranged between .50 and .68 crowns, in Transdanubia between .90 and 1.15 crowns, in the three counties of the Stormy Corner (Békés, Csanád, and Csongrád) they varied between 1.83 and 2.07 crowns per day in 1890,[69] and while in "feudal" Transdanubia medium and latifundiary estates occupied 50–75

---

[68] Bunzel, *op. cit.*, p. 19.

[69] Pál Sándor, "Die Agrarkrise in Ungarn," *Studia Historica* (Budapest) Vol. LI (1954), 189.

per cent of arable land, in Békés small proprietors owned 63.7 per cent of all land.[70] Yet it was also in the Stormy Corner where market economy and wage labor made the deepest inroads into rural life, and where the disorganization of traditional social structures had progressed furthest. While most of the peasantry of Transdanubia lived as cottagers (*zsellér*) on large estates in a condition of semiserfdom and misery but within a relatively secure and predictable pattern of life, those of the Stormy Corner had been transformed into a free-floating labor force at the mercy of seasonal demand and the vagaries of the international grain market. Another source of frustration, peculiar to the Stormy Corner, was a temporary spurt in the labor force in the 1880's when a large number of poor peasants had been employed as navvies with the construction of canals and dams, and later found it hard to readjust to the conditions of farm labor.

The connection between social mobilization and the riots was observed by a number of contemporaries. Investigating the causes of the crisis the Liberal Lajos Návay stated that "the material conditions of the laborers in the Plainland are far superior to those elsewhere in the country," thus "the origins of the movement are not economic but social. . . . Its causes are to be found in the values and ideas of the laborers."[71] The conservative deputy, Gedeon Rohonczy, explained the unrest in these terms: "Twenty years ago we had social peace. But twenty years ago we had no railroad and telegraph. The peasant went about his business and associated with his own kind. For advice he had his lord and priest and he listened to them."[72] The leaders of the

---

[70] *Magyar Statisztikai Szemle*, XXIV (1900), 64.
[71] Lajos Návay, "Az alföldi munkáskérdes" (The Problem of Laborers in the Plainland), *Budapesti Szemle*, IV (1895), 36 and 39.
[72] *Napló* (1898), XII, 392.

riotous peasants interpreted the causes of dissatisfaction in similar terms. Answering the investigating committee of the local lord lieutenant, one Albert Szilágyi stated: "The rightful demands of the laborers had increased because the people of the land study more, know more, see more. How can you blame us? We have learnt how to read and write. We would now like to wear better clothes, eat like human beings and send our children to the schools."[73]

The attitude of the governments toward the agricultural movements was dictated as much by ideology as by pragmatic economic and political considerations. Like the Marxists, nineteenth-century liberals regarded the peasantry as a declining social class and its political manifestations as passing phenomena. In this view the peasantry was a retrogressive force doomed by history, thus it was not necessary to find longterm adjustments with it. In economic terms, an increase of agrarian wages was seen as a direct threat to the marginal profit rates of agricultural enterprise and its ability to modernize production. Finally, the physically dispersed and ill-organized peasantry was far weaker than the industrial proletariat, and its movements were far easier to suppress. Thus the same István Tisza who was the chief advocate of "paying off" the industrial proletariat, vehemently protested the idea that similar policies might apply to the agricultural labor force.[74] Consequently, each of the social insurance laws and other measures designed to alleviate the condition of the lower classes explicitly excluded the rural proletariat. Also, at the same time when the urban workers' right to bargain was restored, various legislative acts restricted the nature of contractual relationships and banned strikes in the agricultural sector. The Agricultural Labor

---

[73] Andor Vadnay, *A Tiszamellékről* (About the Tisza-River Region), (Budapest: Budapesti Hirlap, 1900), p. 27.

[74] See especially his speech in *Napló* (1895), III, 379.

Acts of 1898 and 1907 (sometimes dubbed as Slave Labor Acts) established a kind of neoserfdom by declaring labor contracts inviolable, making incitement to strike a felony punishable by heavy prison sentences, and providing that all fugitive laborers found in breach of contract should be returned to the landowner by the gendarmerie.

From the point of view of the governments, the problem of mass politics was aggravated by the circumstance that some 50 per cent (Table IV) of the potential "public"

Table IV. THE ETHNIC STRUCTURE OF HUNGARY, 1880 TO 1910

	1880	1890	1900	1910
Magyar	46.6	48.5	51.4	54.5
German	13.6	13.1	11.8	10.4
Slovak	13.5	12.5	11.9	10.7
Rumanian	17.5	17.1	16.7	16.1
Ruthenians	2.6	2.5	2.5	2.5
Serbo-Croats	4.6	4.6	3.7	3.6
Other	1.6	1.7	2.0	2.2

SOURCE: Lajos Lóczy, *A magyar szentkorona országainak léirása* (Survey of the Countries of the Hungarian Crown), (Budapest, 1918), p. 173.

were members of "national minorities," the official designation for the non-Magyar inhabitants of the country. The latter became a "problem" first in the early nineteenth century when overzealous Hungarian nation builders abolished Latin (until then used for official announcements) and attempted to replace it with their own. Initially this was merely a design to create a common language of communication in the place of a DEAD language associated with medieval society and institutions, but in later years Hungarian leaders began to adapt a more intolerant policy of drawing disparate ethnic groups into a homogeneous national community. Thus in the seventies and eighties Mag-

yar nationalists were no longer content to spread a common language but insisted on cultural assimilation. "Since
patriotism is inconceivable without a common language,"
said one of the exponents of the official Hungarian point
of view in 1882, "our task is to create one. However, we
expect not only that they speak Magyar, but also that they
identify and feel with Magyardom. This we expect, and
if they reject our outstretched hands we will have to use
methods that in the short run will not be able to generate
much confidence but in the long run will produce effective
results." [75] These objectives were to be attained by an "educational offensive," that is, by spreading literacy, introducing Magyar as a subject of instruction in private schools,
and using it as the language of instruction in schools supported or maintained by the state. The thrust of these
policies was to be at the level of institutions of higher learning which one Magyar nationalist (himself a recent convert
to Magyardom) aptly described as a "big machine . . . you
feed in a Slovak kid on the one side, and on the other out
comes a Hungarian gentleman." [76]

Throughout the period the governments, aided by
significant segments of the Magyar public, used methods
of the carrot and the stick. On the one hand, the recal-
citrant were harassed, subjected to vilification, and hauled
into the courts of law to be tried by Magyar juries. On the
other hand, those who were willing to accept the language
and culture of the dominant ethnic group, were accepted
with open arms and received preferential treatment in all
walks of life. Well aware that assimilation was ineffectual

---

[75] Quoted in József Sándor, *Az E.M.K.E. megalapítása* (The Foundation of the Transylvanian Magyar Cultural League), (Kolozsvár:
Emke, 1910), pp. 83–84.
[76] Béla Grünwald, *A Felvidék* (The Highlands), (Budapest: Ráth
Mov, 1878), p. 140.

short of material and social incentives[77] the bureaucracy, the principal avenue of social mobility in the country, thrust open its gates to talented German, Slovak, and Rumanian youth on the tacit condition that they renounce their ethnic origins and adapt the style and values of the Hungarian upper class. In a remarkable gesture the gentry accepted all comers, and by the end of the century it transformed the bureaucracy into one of the principal social agents of national assimilation and social integration. "New elements," writes an unfriendly observer of the old regime, "either by becoming ennobled or simply by conforming to the caste mind, were with certain limitations admitted to the [ruling] class, provided they not only unreservedly recognized the basic theory but also attempted to assimilate the dubious morality of the so-called 'historical classes.' . . . . In Hungary, a potential middle-class was absorbed by a gradually degenerating nobility. Because of the vagueness of the gentry concept, it was the recognition of a newcomer as 'one of us' by those who were members by birth that really mattered." [78] This trend is clearly reflected in the changing ethnic composition of public administration. While at the turn of the century 92.9 per cent of local officials, 95.6 per cent of the ministerial bureaucracy, and 96.9 per cent of all judges listed themselves as Magyars in the official census,[79] an analysis of family names shows an increasing proportion of public officials recruited from the non-Magyar element. Between 1890 and 1910 the percentage of the gentry among senior officials in the Ministry of

[77] An interesting statement to this effect may be found in Dezsö Bánffy, *Magyar nemzetiségi politika* (Hungarian Nationality Policies), Budapest: Légrády, 1903), p. 143.
[78] Rusztem Vámbéry, *Hungary: To Be Or Not To Be* (New York: Ungar, 1946), p. 79.
[79] *Hungarian Peace Negotiations*, I, 236–237.

the Interior declined from 64.1 per cent to 45.6 per cent, in the Ministry of Finance from 53.8 to 38.6 per cent. At the same time the percentage of foreign names increased from 21.8 to 38.2 per cent in the Ministry of the Interior and from 37.1 to 48.8 per cent in the Ministry of Finance.[80] The consequences of this pattern of recruitment became even more fully evident in the interwar period when (in 1930) 35.5 per cent of the names of senior officials in the Ministry of Defense, 47.1 per cent in Education, 51.8 per cent in the Foreign Office, and 37.2 to 44.9 per cent in the other departments pointed to non-Magyar origin.[81] Gradually the gentry elite was being transformed into a "gentroid" or, less pejoratively, "seignorial" (*úri*) middle class, a bureaucratic element that was plebeian in origin but patrician in its social pretensions. At the same time, the minorities were being deprived of much of their potential leadership. This fact is strikingly demonstrated in the prewar statistical breakdown of the educated classes. According to the census of 1910 Rumanians made up 16.1 per cent of the population, Slovaks 10.7 per cent, and Ruthenians 2.5 per cent, while the corresponding percentages of high-school graduates who professed to be members of these ethnic groups were 3.4, 1.1, and .1 per cent.[82]

As these policies indicate, the gentroid-bureaucratic state was not insensitive to the problems of social mobilization and attempted to meet the challenge by providing economic rewards and avenues of social mobility to the ascendant classes in lieu (or perhaps in preparation) of

---

[80] Based on members of the executive class, (fogalmazói kar) as they appear in Magyar Királyi Statisztikai Hivatal, *Magyarország Tiszti Cím és Névtára* for 1890 and 1910.

[81] Lakatos, *op. cit.*, pp. 72–73.

[82] *Hungarian Peace Negotiations*, III, 213.

political participation. These policies, however, failed mainly because the weaknesses of the economy and the scarcity of available resources placed significant limitations on the capacity of the system to "pay off" strategic groups among the politically relevant population. While the mobilization of society proceeded at a relatively high rate (considerably accelerated by nationalist cultural policies), economic development was retarded by conditions that were outside the control of governments, most significantly by a protracted and devastating agricultural price depression in the last quarter of the nineteenth century. The industrialization of the country finally got under way around 1900, and as a result *per capita* national income increased by 74 per cent between 1901 and 1913; but in absolute figures this merely represented an increase from 185 to 325 crowns or $37 to $65.[83]

In addition to the objective condition of scarcity, the stability of the political system was adversely affected by the perennial problem of underdeveloped countries, the condition of relative deprivation engendered by the so-called international demonstration effect. Through the intermediary function of the international Socialist movement urban labor had been exposed to conditions prevailing in the more advanced industrial societies and their aspirations became heavily influenced by consumption patterns and real wages in the latter. The leaders of the workers, together with other critics of Hungarian society, painted a gloomy picture of working-class life contrasting the condition of the Hungarian laborer with his counterparts in Austria, Germany, or Britain, and blaming the ruling classes for the existing differences. To be sure, these dif-

---

[83] Frigyes Fellner, *Magyarország nemzeti jövedelme* (The National Income of Hungary), (Budapest: Akadémiai Nyomda, 1916).

ferences were striking enough and far more depressed than anywhere in the industrial West. But neither the critics nor the workers ever attempted to compare Hungary with Russia, Bulgaria, or Rumania, or else place the wage differentials in the perspective of national income and wealth. While the critics denounce Hungarian conditions and point out that real wages in industry were 80 per cent of the Austrian, 70 per cent of German, and less than half of the British, they rarely state that *per capita* income in Hungary was less than 50 per cent of Austria's, 27 per cent of Germany's, and only 16 per cent of Great Britain's.[84] The failure to appreciate this perspective made it difficult, if not impossible, to satisfy the industrial proletariat with the meager spoils that the Hungarian economy could offer at the height of the industrial revolution and integrate the urban masses into a political system based on pragmatic bargaining over the rational distribution of social resources.

The politics of scarcity created agonizing dilemmas for governments, because a policy designed to satisfy some group was bound to alienate another. Thus after the industrial reforms of 1899-1904 designed to "pay off" the working class, the bourgeoisie visibly cooled toward the bureaucratic state and quietly began to search for political alternatives.[85] The same was also true concerning the aristocracy. Even though the landed classes were far less affected by the wage policies of the government than the industrial entrepreneurs after the turn of the century, they increasingly came to the conclusion that the protection provided by the bureaucratic machine was inadequate. In 1905 the landed aristocracy not only broke with István Tisza and

---

[84] See Molnár, *op. cit.*, pp. 176 and 192.

[85] Striking evidence for this appears in a secret report addressed by the Minister of the Interior to the King in 1906. See Gratz, *op. cit.*, II, 93.

the Liberals but entered into a coalition with nationalist radicals in search for a better political "deal." After the fiasco of this coalition, most big landowners, like the big bourgeoisie, reentered Tisza's new government party, though some conservative stalwarts stayed on the opposition and joined the Independents and Forty-eighters in the filibuster of 1912, only to be dragged out and bodily ejected from parliament upon Tisza's orders.

Economic limitations also interfered with the process of absorbing upward mobile groups into the bureaucratic machine. In the last decade of the nineteenth and the first decade of the twentieth century the civil service was expanded beyond all rational, administrative need (the employees of the state increased from 16,000 in 1866 to 60,776 in 1890 and 119,937 in 1910)[86] making the salary of public officials the single largest item in the budget. But even so, public administration and professional politics were not able to satisfy all comers. To use a popular Hungarian saying, "too many were the Eskimo and too few the seals." In order to accommodate the intelligentsia of the minorities many applicants of gentry origin had to be turned away. These frustrated candidates became bitter and implacable foes of the regime, and their presence gave parliamentary politics an increasingly turbulent character. Thus between 1899 and 1905 the parties of the dispossessed gentry for all practical purposes paralyzed the political process by a series of vicious technical filibusters. Then in 1906 the Independence and Forty-eight parties (temporarily united) finally made their way to power and tried to reap all the benefits that public office could offer. During the three and a half years of the coalition government tens of thousands of erst-

---

[86] Károly Keleti, *Hazánk és népe* (Our Country and People), (Budapest: Ráth Mór, 1889), p. 55. *Annuaire Stastistique Hongois,* IX (1901), 80, and XIX (1911), 93.

while loyal supporters made their pilgrimage to the capital, and 22,000 of them (many presumably of the declining gentry) were given employment with the state.[87] Those who did not "make it" during these years lost hope and became convinced that it was impossible for them to work effectively within the system. From 1910 on the left wing of the national opposition, first under the leadership of Gyula Justh, then under Mihály Károlyi, gave up any pretense of loyal opposition to the Tisza machine, and began to collaborate with the Socialists and the national minorities as one of the champions of universal suffrage. In 1918, the Károlyi faction of the party became the standard bearer, and later the Gironde, of the ill-fated democratic revolution.

These economic limitations weighed even more heavily on the intelligentsia that had sprung up from the commercial and industrial classes. Throughout the period the Jewish bourgeoisie displayed an exceptionally high level of educational mobility. Jews as a group were far more literate than the rest of the population (57.7 per cent as opposed to 36.1 in 1869, and 74.7 to 58.2 in 1910)[88] and persons of the Jewish faith represented a disproportionately high percentage of students enrolled in institutions of higher learning. (In 1883, 19 per cent of the students of gymnasiums,

[87] To illustrate the dilemmas of bureaucratic recruitment and its political implications we may note that the massive influx of the gentry in 1906–1910 created instant repercussions among the national minorities. As Seton-Watson observed in 1908: "A new stage has been reached when the renegades or Magyarones, as they are called, are no longer welcome, and when competition is embittered by the overproduction of the educated class. And as this corresponds with a genuine economic revival among the non-Magyars, those who would have been turncoats a generation ago, find fewer openings and a colder reception than their predecessors and are thus tempted to remain true to their nationality" (Seton-Watson, *op. cit.*, p. 211).

[88] Kovács, *op. cit.*, p. 40.

34.6 per cent of realgymnasiums [practical course], and 46.1 per cent of commercial schools were Jewish; in 1913 the figures were 16.9, 38.0, and 57.4 per cent).[89] The economic system was not well enough developed to absorb all the available trained personnel, and the middle-class intelligentsia began to gravitate toward political roles. In 1910 we will already find that 4.9 per cent of the employees in the central state bureaucracy, 3 per cent in the counties, 6.1 per cent of municipal officials, and 4.8 per cent of the judges were Jewish.[90] As to the House of Representatives, the Hungarian Jewish Encyclopedia lists 50 Jewish members for the entire Compromise Era.[91]

Even greater was the number of converted Jews in Hungarian political life. Thus, according to one source there were 26 members of Jewish ancestry in the parliament of 1906–1910[92] and perhaps twice as many in the last House of Representatives (1910–1918). At the same time, individuals of Jewish parentage were occupying the Cabinet portfolios for Finance, Trade and National Defense, and the office of the Lord Mayor of Budapest. The ethnic division of labor carefully and implicitly established in the nineteenth century, was breaking down creating new opportunities and new social tensions. Yet Jewish participation in administration and politics, although not disproportionately small, never encompassed more than a fraction of potential recruits, most of them from the upper classes, whereas the educated offspring of lower and lower-middle class families wer forced to seek a career elsewhere, usually in the professions, arts, and mass communications

---

[89] *Ibid.*

[90] *Magyar Tájékoztató zusebkönyv* (Hungarian Information Almanac), (Budapest: Magyar Nemzeti Szövetseg, 1943), p. 57.

[91] *Magyar zsidó lexikon*, p. 911.

[92] Seton-Watson, *op. cit.*, p. 188.

(meaning journalism in those days). This group was politically highly competent but socially marginal, wedged between economic and political elites yet belonging to neither. Frustrated by their marginality they repudiated both the gentry and the bourgeois value systems and sought new social purpose in mass political leadership. In time they became the main reservoir of Hungary's radical intelligentsia and provided the bulk of Socialist and Communist elites in the coming revolutions.

If conditions of economic backwardness and scarcity created critical social discontinuities, the traditional symbols of state authority further exacerbated the crisis by providing a convenient target for criticism and a catalyst for the diverse forces of the radical opposition. The greatest weakness of the old regime was not, as its critics are wont to charge, that it was inflexible, incompetent, and insensitive to contingencies created by modernization but that, despite its considerable flexibility and openness, it projected an image of uncompromising rigidity. The political establishment remained haughtily gentry and Magyar in name when in reality it was neither. In fact, the Hungarian establishment was open to both non-Magyars and plebeians, but when one outsider began his climb on the social ladder he was forced to repudiate his origins and pretend that he was the scion of an old, noble family. Instead of proudly advertising its openness to popular talent, and thereby arguing for its legitimacy in the modern world, the Hungarian elite attempted to derive moral and political strength from its pseudo-exclusiveness cloaking its equitable features in the disguise of ostentatious contempt for achievement. Similarly, there was something appallingly anachronistic, not so much in the denial of political participation to the masses, but in the way this was justified by the innate qualifications of the "historical classes" at a time when the latter were already being replaced by a new class, historical in its pretensions but not in its social origins.

Such anachronistic symbols and rationalizations only deepened the abyss between rulers and ruled, and raised anguished outcries against a "medieval" political order. If the gentry ethos did not interfere with the short-term rationality of bureaucratic solutions, in the long run it was responsible for the breakdown of communications between the upper and lower echelons of society. In the last analysis, it was this breakdown of communication that allowed the ascendancy of new elites who were neither more humane, nor more democratic than the gentry, but were more skillful in manipulating the symbols of modern politics. Under the slogans of equity and fraternity that the gentry had found so hard to utter, the radical intelligentsia would draw the most frustrated and mobilized classes into a new political community only to press society into the more ruthless and efficient mold of the "dictatorship of the proletariat" that emerged out of the forthcoming revolutions.

2

Coalition Politics in the Hungarian Soviet Republic

Peter Kenez

CONTEMPORARIES called the Hungarian Soviet Republic the Béla Kun regime, historians sometimes refer to it as the Hungarian Communist Republic, but both observers and participants have always agreed that it was the Communists who determined the main outlines of policy. Socialist memoirists, of course, use phrases different from the Communists to describe their own junior status: they say they only participated in the government "in order to save as much as possible out of the achievements of the October Revolution" [1] and "to humanize the regime" while the Communists write that the role of their coalition partners was merely that of wreckers and saboteurs. There is general agreement in historical literature about the fact that the regime was basically Communist, and that there were profound disagreements and constant quarrels between the two participating parties.

---

[1] Vilmos Böhm, *Két forradalom tüzében (In the Crossfire of Two Revolutions)*, (Vienna: Bécsi Magyar Kiadó, 1923), p. 261. ". . . we stayed on the commanding bridge of the ship which was battered by the storm, to save with one great effort, which could be saved."

In spite of the unanimity, there is something suspicious about this picture. How could the Communists, possessing only a few thousand adherents and having formed their party only four months before, dominate the Socialists, who were in secure control of the trade-union movement, their party having hundreds of thousands of members and sympathizers and organizations of long continuity? One must remember that Béla Kun was the only Communist commissar out of twelve in the government formed on March 21, 1919.[2] Why would Social Democratic leaders carry out a policy contrary to their ideas?

The interpretation which will be developed here is that the disagreements between the two parties have been exaggerated. For contemporaries, including the leaders, distinction between socialism and communism was not as clear as it is to us. Communism was in a state of becoming. Even in Russia, where Lenin's purposeful leadership first created those features which we later came to associate with communism, Bolshevism was still in a state of flux, and it had little to do with the party it was to become in the 1930's. Lenin established the Comintern in March 1919 for the explicit purpose of splitting international socialism and imposing the Russian model on at least part of the European Left. The period of the Hungarian Soviet Republic coincided with the time of realignment of the international labor movement.

There is no sharp line between Communists and Socialists; in fact, the usefulness of such labels in this period can be questioned. The Left-Socialist program—and only the Left and Center participated in the coalition—did not call for substantially different policies from those which the Communists wanted. This is not to say that there were no

---

[2] Because the Commissariat for Agriculture was headed by a five-man college including one Communist, Károly Vántus, one might say that there were two Communist commissars.

factional struggles, but these were not between two well-defined groups with developed ideological positions.

If this interpretation is correct, then why did the history of the coalition come to be distorted? It happened because historians and memoirists portrayed communism in 1919 not as it was but as it would become, and projected a later ideological split into a period when it did not yet exist. Also, there is an all-too-human desire to find scapegoats. Instead of admitting, which seems rather obvious to us, that the government fell because of the strength and determination of foreign enemies, the Socialists have preferred to think that the cause of defeat was Communist extremism, blind imitation of an irrelevant Russian model, and bad strategy pursued by the Communist leaders, whereas the Communists have attributed its failure to treason among their allies.

Curiously, later political necessities made Socialist and Communist interests coincide in emphasizing past disagreements. Many Socialists, by believing and advertising that they had played only secondary roles in the Soviet Republic, could return to Horthy's Hungary and take up "respectable" positions. Instead of remembering the few feverish months when once in their lives they acted according to the principles in which they professed to believe, that is, like revolutionaries, they preferred to stress that they had been the first to fight the Communists. The memoirs of two prominent Socialist leaders, Jakab Weltner and Vilmos Böhm, show the contradiction: we are told that the Socialists were powerless and yet we are presented with numerous examples of Socialist strength as we learn how Socialists successfully asserted themselves in the service of some good cause against the followers of Béla Kun.[3]

---

[3] Böhm, op. cit., and Jakab Weltner, *Forradalom, bolsevizmus, emigráció (Revolution, Bolshevism, Emigration),* (Budapest: Weltner, 1929).

On the other hand, the Communist exiles were not reticent in claiming credit for the defeated experiment. In Communist circles, unlike Socialist groups, even a defeated revolution conferred prestige on the participants. Béla Kun liked to boast that he had ruled over one of the very few Communist regimes in the world.[4]

Since 1919, Communist literature has dealt tirelessly with the "lessons" of the Hungarian Soviet Republic, and the chief lesson usually seems to be that real revolutionaries must not cooperate with Socialist traitors. When in 1920, at the Second Congress of the Communist International, the Russians forced the twenty-one conditions on the participating parties and thereby made the split between international communism and the Socialist movement final, they used the argument that 1919 in Hungary "proved" that Communists should not share power with Socialists.[5] However, this is putting the carriage before the horse, for from their perspective the Bolsheviks needed no new proof that the Socialists were treacherous. The decision to split the international labor movement was made independently of the Hungarian experience and only after, and in the light of this decision, the history of the Hungarian Soviet Republic was written.

It was ironic that it was in Hungary, of all countries of Europe, where a genuine coalition of socialist parties was achieved, for the Hungarian Social Democratic party had been among the most reformist and revisionist. The Social

[4] Communists in exile had time to compose pamphlets about the experience of the "glorious" 133 days. The attitude of Kun and others can be best summarized as "defeat strengthens character." See the collection of Kun's writing, Béla Kun, *A Magyar Tanácsköztársaságról* On the Hungarian Soviet Republic, (Budapest: Kossuth, 1958).

[5] This point of view is accepted even by some Western scholars. See for example David Cattel, "The Hungarian Revolution of 1919 and the Reorganization of the Comintern in 1920," *Journal of Central European Affairs* XI (January-April 1951), 27–38.

Democratic party had been an organization of trade unions where membership in a union automatically meant membership in the party and where the party was led by former workers who gained experience in trade-union work and had little interest in ideology or political theory. Although, of course, in words they accepted a Marxist, revolutionary, and internationalist ideology, in practice they were content to fight for improvement of working conditions and increase of wages, and in politics they raised their sights no higher than the achievement of universal suffrage. Whatever radicalism there was in the working classes—and the strikes and street fighting of 1907 and 1912 were serious enough to terrify the Hungarian bourgeoisie—it was in spite of and not because of its Socialist leadership.

Because of the organizational peculiarities of the party, the Left was so weak and so poorly represented in the leadership that the reformists could easily isolate it. When the Left attempted to fight back and to appeal to international Socialist authorities, in 1910 thirty-one leaders of the opposition, headed by Gyula Alpári, were excluded from the party.[6] Jakab Weltner, the editor of the party paper, *Népszava*, could boast in February 1918 that the Hungarian party was among the very few which did not split during the war.[7] The reason for this "unity" was that whatever Marxist, revolutionary elements existed in Hungary, existed outside of the Socialist party, forming loosely organized, rather powerless

---

[6] Tibor Szamuely, *A Kommunisták Magyarországi Pártjának megalakulása és harca a Proletárdiktatúraert (The Founding of the Hungarian Communist Party and Its Struggle for the Dictatorship of the Proletariat)*, (Budapest: Kossuth, 1964), p. 42. The radicals were mostly intellectuals. Most of them were to play important roles in the founding of the Communist party and in the Soviet Republic, for example Gyula Alpári, László Rudas, Béla Szántó, Jenö László, Béla Vágó, and Artúr Illés.

[7] Weltner in *Népszava*, February 12, 1918.

little groups from which ultimately the bolshevized prisoners of war, returning from Russia, succeeded in forming the Hungarian Communist party in November, 1918.

The factional struggle within the prewar Social Democratic party was to have significant consequences for the working of the coalition in the Soviet Republic. The highhanded methods of the reformist leadership and the Left's appeal to the International left such bitter and personal animosities that cooperation or even normal social intercourse was difficult. The Social Democratic leaders much preferred to deal with such Moscow-trained men as Béla Kun and Károly Vántus, who had been little known to them before the war than with their former comrades, Alpári, Béla Szántó, Béla Vágó, and László Rudas.[8]

After the defeat of the monarchy in World War I, the liberal-democratic Mihály Károlyi formed a government in Budapest in which the Socialists accepted two portfolios. The Communist party, which soon came into being, aimed at bringing down this government with which the Socialists were associated. The soil for disruptive propaganda was extremely fertile, and the strength and influence of the newly formed Communist party grew amazingly quickly. It is impossible to establish to what extent the Communists created and to what extent they merely profited from disorganization. The country faced such enormous problems that a government based on democratic principles was not likely to be able to cope with them. Anarchy was rapidly approaching.

Under the pressure of events, the Social Democratic party moved to the left; nevertheless, the party lost a sub-

---

[8] Weltner, *op. cit.*, pp. 156–157. For example, after the unification the Communists named Alpári to be their representative at the editorial office of *Népszava*. Weltner threatened with resignation and therefore the Communists sent Elek Bolgár instead of Alpári.

stantial part of the radicalized workers to the Communists. At first, the Socialists regarded their competitors among the workers as merely a nuisance, but soon they found it necessary to fight back: the Socialist-dominated workers' council expelled the Communist faction, and Socialist ministers supported police measures against their fellow Marxists. The *Népszava* called the Communists splitters and criminals and referred to them as Communists only in quotation marks. Anticommunism also implied antisovietism. Weltner did not want to publish Lenin's telegram to the Hungarian workers on the occasion of the October Revolution in the party paper,[9] and Böhm was instrumental in sending munitions to the Ukrainians fighting Lenin's regime.[10]

The Communists reciprocated in kind. They attacked the Socialists where it hurt most by pointing to the differences between the Socialists' avowed belief in revolution and their antirevolutionary behavior. The struggle culmiated on February 20 in a Communist-inspired demonstration in front of *Népszava* where six people died and sixty were wounded. As a result of this demonstration the government imprisoned Béla Kun and sixty-seven other Communist leaders. It seemed that the gap between the Socialists and Communists was so great that it could never be bridged.

The Károlyi regime was becoming increasingly powerless when on March 20 the *Entente* demanded the acceptance of borders profundly unjust to the Hungarians. What a shock this development must have been to the Hungarian people can best be seen by its immediate political results: the government could neither accept the demands nor organize the country to fight against them. Only one course

[9] Weltner, *op. cit.*, p. 76.
[10] Anonymous, *Tisztelt Szovjet (Respected Soviet)*, (Budapest, 1919), p. 15.

was open to it—resignation. In the crisis, the non-Marxist parties could not accept responsibility; power fell into the hands of the Social Democrats who invited the Communists to unite their parties and participate in the creation of a new regime.

The unification took place entirely on the basis of the Communist program, but the new government had an almost exclusively Socialist leadership. With the exception of Béla Kun, all commissars were Socialists. However, the Communist victory in getting acceptance for the program and the Socialist victory in the choice of leadership should not be exaggerated: the Communist program coincided in many instances with the wishes of the Socialists; a large part of the program remained a dead letter or became significantly modified in practice; above all, the Socialists had nothing to offer in its place. On the other hand, Socialist domination of the government was not as complete as it appeared: every commissar had a deputy, who came from the opposite party. Since the deputies had also one vote each in the Revolutionary Governing Council, one might say that every Commissariat had two leaders, a Socialist and a Communist. Ironically, it was the Communists, freshly out of jail, who tried to persuade their recent enemies to take posts in the government.[11] The Communists, with the exception of Kun, were unknown in the country, and the government needed the prestige which the old labor leaders still possessed among the workers.

The workers, who never understood the depth and causes of the quarrels between the two Marxist parties, greeted the realization of Socialist unity with enthusiasm. However, the unification was such a startling reversal of the tactics of the two parties that it was inevitable that many

---

[11] Böhm, *op. cit.*, p. 262.

among the leaders, who had been responsible for the previous tactics, would approach each other with suspicions and
that some, in both parties, would find it impossible to go
along with the new policy. Why did the Socialist and Communist leaders make such a volte-face? How honest were
they in seeking unity?

For Communist historians the agreement presented two
separate issues: forming a coalition government and amal-
gamating the two parties.[12] None of the historians, including those who considered the Socialist traitors, faulted Kun
for joining the government. After all, Lenin, albeit under
different circumstances, accepted a coalition with Left Social Revolutionaries. Kun, however has been blamed for
abolishing an independent Communist party, because unification in practice meant the absorption of the much smaller
party into the other.

The Communists could reject the Socialist offer to join
the government only if they believed in the possibility of a
successful uprising. Indeed, there were some who worked
for such a goal. The so-called Second Central Committee of
the Party, that is, the leaders who took the place of their
jailed comrades, made preparations without the knowledge
of Kun for a new revolution. But Kun was far too realistic
to believe in the possibility of a successful takeover. He
understood that the chances of keeping, as opposed to taking, power, were close to zero, because the Communists did
not have the necessary organization and they did not even
have enough reliable and competent men to fill the ministries. Unlike some of his followers, he did not let himself
be misled by the Russian example and realized that the
Hungarian Social Democratic leaders had greater support

[12] See for example, Tibor Hajdu, "A Magyar Tanácsköztársaság történetének néhány kérdéséhez" (On some questions of the history of
the Hungarian Soviet Republic) *Századok,* 92, nos. 1–4 (1958).

among the workers than the Mensheviks could have counted on in Russia in 1917. Therefore, he felt that the only way the Party could come to power in Hungary was in conjunction with the Socialists.

Many members of the Second Central Committee disapproved of Kun's decision. But they did so only partly for fear of compromising their revolutionary purity; their chief reason was that Kun handled the negotiations in a high-handed manner excluding those comrades who had not been in jail with him. Kun's lack of tact in handling the crucial issue of unification contained the germs of later dissension.

No one among the Communists (and only Zsigmond Kunfi among the Socialists)[13] suggested at the unification meeting that the parties should retain their independent existence and join only for the purpose of forming a government. The ease with which they sacrificed their organization followed from the Hungarian Communists' concept of the Party, which was more Luxemburgist than Leninist. The ideas prevalent on this crucial issue among the Communists show that it would be anachronistic to think of the Hungarian Party at that time as a Bolshevist organization. Béla Kun had little understanding of Leninist ideology, and the theoreticians had not yet freed themselves from their Western European revolutionary Socialist background.

György Lukács, who because of his emphasis on humanism and "democratic dictatorship" was considered to be on the right wing of the party, and László Rudas, who was a leader of the left wing, agreed with Luxemburg's ideas of spontaneity. According to Lukács, the proletariat needed a party only in the period of transition, when the class consciousness of workers was still insufficiently developed, at a time when the proletariat was already too strong to with-

---

[13] *Ibid.*, p. 376.

draw from political life, yet not strong enough to dominate it. In his view, proletarian dictatorship created genuine unity among workers, which made party in the old sense useless. The new party was to be the executive organ of the victorious proletariat.[14] Interestingly, the left-wing Rudas went even further in denigrating the role of the party. Footnoting Luxemburg's *Mass strike*, he wrote that parties played only secondary roles in revolutions, for on these occasions it was precisely the least organized elements of the working classes which acquired crucial importance.[15]

The Communists and the left-wing Socialists drew from the same ideological source and this fact made them more willing to work together. The Communists accepted the merger because they believed that the Socialists adopting the program had capitulated, and it did not occur to them that maintaining an independent organization might prove useful in later disputes and struggles.

It is harder to understand what motivated the Socialists to search for a compromise with their opponents. Power fell into their hands; the Communists were not in a position to threaten it seriously. However, the Social Democratic politicians who never freed themselves from a trade-unionist mentality had an ambiguous attitude toward power: on the one hand, they felt they did not have the moral right to

---

[14] On Lukács' view of the party in 1919, see above all "Taktik und Ethik" in P. Ludz. ed., *Georg Lukács: Schriften zur Ideologie und Politik* (Berlin: Luchterhand, 1967), also see Lukács' introduction to the translation of Rosa Luxemburg, *Tömegsztrájk* (Mass Strike), (Budapest: Közoktatási Népbiztosság Kiadása, 1919); and "A proletáregység helyreállitásának elméleti jelentösége" (The Theoretical Significance of the Recreation of the Working Class Unity) in Jakab Weltner ed., *Az Egység Okmányai* (The Documents of Unity) (Budapest: Közoktatási Népbiztosság Kiadása, 1919).

[15] László Rudas, "Lényeg és forma" (Essence and Form), *Internationale*, I, 6–7 (1919), 1–6.

relinquish it, since they alone had some organized following; on the other, they dreaded the responsibility of governing the country alone. As long as they could find allies
among the "bourgeois" parties, they cooperated with them,
and when this became impossible, they turned to the Communists.

One of the chief motivations of the Social Democrats
was nationalism. They found the *Entente* terms, as expressed in the Vyx note of March 20, as outrageous as all
other Hungarians found them.[16] It was the democratic states
of Western Europe which produced the Vyx note, causing
the Socialists to make an emotional break with the West.
They thus felt justified in turning to the only fighting op-
ponent of the *Entente*, Soviet Russia. The Socialists believed that the price of Russian help would be the offer of
at least a share of the power to the Communists. Also, the
country, and above all the working classes, had to be organized for an armed struggle, and the Socialists believed that
this would be impossible without Communist help. To
some extent they were the victims of their own propaganda:
as they saw the radicalization of the workers and their own
decreasing authority over them, they imagined the change
of mood to be the result of Communist agitation; believing
that as they lost followers, the Communists gained them.
This was only partly true, because although the Communists could undoubtedly cause trouble, it was uncertain
whether they could also exercise control over the workers.
The Socialists formed a government for the purpose of fighting the foreign enemy—it seemed impossible to them to
fight the domestic enemies at the same time.

After unification, the Socialists justified their move to
their followers and to themselves by playing down the dif-

---

[16] See for example Böhm, *op. cit.*, pp. 238–250.

ferences which had existed between them and the Communists. For example, Weltner, in his introduction to the published documents of unification, maintained that the two parties could come together because there had been no ideological differences between them. They had differed only on the question of speed in introducing the revolutionary reforms. But even here, he claimed, the difference had not been substantial: the Socialists would have liked to increase the tempo, but their "bourgeois" allies in the government prevented them.[17] One could dismiss these and similar statements as propaganda, yet, one suspects, at least temporarily the Socialists really believed in them and imagined their past to be more revolutionary than it was.

In view of the extreme bitterness of the struggle between the two parties before March 21, the chances for the success of collaboration were not good. Yet the unification succeeded—if by success we understand that the Communists and Socialists during the era of the Soviet Republic never faced each other as hostile blocs. Only a single incident occurred in this period when former Communists and former Socialists took positions on the basis of old alignments: in the June Party congress the Socialists fought for the name of the party to be "Party of Hungarian Socialists" and the Communists insisted on "Party of Hungarian Communists." Finally, they sensibly compromised on "Party of Hungarian Socialist-Communist Workers." The issue generated much heat and some bitterness, but it was still only of minor symbolic significance. The debate was caused not by Communists and Socialists recommending different policies but by the desire of politicians to remain faithful to their previous positions and prove themselves victorious by the choice of name. Even on this issue prominent former

---

[17] Jakab Weltner, "Bevezetés" (Introduction) in Jakab Weltner ed., *Az Egység Okmányai (The Documents of Unity)*.

Socialists (for example the great orator of the party, Dezsö Bokányi) sided with the Communists. The debate over the name of the party can be regarded as an exception which proves the rule.

A Socialist-Communist confrontation was prevented partly by the prudence of the majority of the leaders, and partly by the minimal cohesion of the two defunct parties. The right wing of the Social Democratic party, which included all vociferous anti-Communists, did not participate in the Soviet regime and became as irrelevant as the bourgeois parties. The left wing, on the other hand, became so closely identified with the Communists that after the defeat many of them ended up in Moscow as members of the reconstituted Communist party. This left the Center, which included some of the most influential leaders, who worked honestly for the survival of the Soviet Republic, and, because they knew that dissension would lead to the victory of counterrevolution, did everything possible to smooth over the differences between Socialists and Communists.

The Communists were also far from united. Those members who had opposed unification came to form a left opposition. With the exception of Tibor Szamuely, who was the leader of this group, and who had been a prisoner of war together with Kun, the group was made up of former Socialists who had the greatest personal dislike for the Social Democrats. Expecially in the first weeks of the regime, the Communist left wing was not without political power: they controlled the political police and one of their adherents, László Rudas, was the editor of *Vörös Újság*, the former Communist paper, which after March 21 became one of the two official organs of the party.

Nothing shows better the skill of Kun's politics than his handling of the Left. He never had unquestioned authority in the party, and Szamuely was a powerful and dangerous rival. Under Szamuely's leadership the Left attacked repeatedly Kun's "opportunistic" policies, who, indeed, made one compromise after another. To defend himself from his leftist critics, the leader of the party had to cover his policies with revolutionary slogans. But Kun knew that the rigidity and dogmatism of the Left was a danger not only to his personal standing in the party but also a danger to the survival of the Soviet Republic. Without doing much harm to the enemies of the regime, the terror had alienated potential supporters; carrying out the adventuristic foreign policy advocated by the Left would have resulted in certain collapse.

At the same time, Kun understood that without the existence of the Left he himself could not long have stayed in power. The Communists were in the government not because they had a large following, but because of extortion: they were strong enough to threaten disturbance and disruption. Kun, knowing the limitations of Communist strength, shaped his policy accordingly: on the one hand he defended the Left, at least to such an extent as to prevent the destruction of this politically useful tool, and on the other, he allowed the Socialists, and at times even encouraged them, to remove the most vociferous representatives of the Left from sensitive positions. For example, Kun went so far as to ask Böhm, the Socialist commissar for war, to request the resignation of Szamuely from his Commissariat, rather than talking personally to his old comrade.[18] Gradually Szamuely's group lost control of the instruments of terror, and he and his followers were sent to the front as political commissars, where they could serve the cause while being excluded from the exercise of real power.

Kun's group, which might be called the Communist Center, was made up of people who had become Commu-

[18] Böhm, *op. cit.*, p. 315.

nists in Russia and who were almost unknown in the country. Even though the public heard less about them than about the noisy followers of Szamuely, they were the ones who exercised political power. The group was characterized by moderation. At times, Kun and his followers tried to find compromises between the Communist Left and the Socialist majority, and thus push the government to the left, but on other occasions they showed less revolutionary determination than the Socialists. For example, Kun had the reputation of being a kind-hearted man, and people persecuted by the regime frequently turned to him for mercy rather than to the Socialists. Communists in the government recommended satisfying the demands of the striking miners,[19] rather than punishing them—and they wanted to wait longer than the Socialists before declaring a territory to be under military law.[20]

Looking at the policies of the regime, it is impossible to determine whether the government pursued a "Socialist" or a "Communist" course. The government existed for only 133 days, and it had to operate constantly in an atmosphere of crisis, when only a limited range of options was open. Under the circumstances the differences in ideology—and these differences have been frequently exaggerated—had little relevance. To illustrate the broad agreement existing in the government on the basic issues, it is worth looking at the handling of the two most controversial issues: agricultural and foreign policies.

A standard feature of Communist memoir literature is the exercise of self-criticism over "incorrect" agricultural policy.[21] Indeed, failure to divide the land, and thereby

---

[19] *Ibid.*, p. 363.

[20] *Ibid.*, p. 362.

[21] See for example articles in Kun, *op. cit.*, and Jenö Varga, Földkérdés a Magyar Proletárforradalomban *(The Land Question in the Hun-*

satisfy the aspirations of the peasantry, contributed to the fall of the Soviet Republic. But the Socialists deserve no less criticism. At the time, there was no debate over agricultural policy, and the Socialists shared the mistaken assumptions of the Communists about the peasants. The leaders of the two parties came from the same social background and had the same prejudice against village life, a prejudice typical of the Central European middle and working classes. This bias was reinforced by Marxist ideology, which underestimated the revolutionary potential of the peasantry and always took the side of the urban against the rural population.

Since its founding in 1890, the Hungarian Social Democratic party had ignored the agrarian question. Up to 1918 it had never called for land reform, for it regarded the destruction of remnants of feudalism as a task of the bourgeoisie, which had nothing to do with the interests of the proletariat. When Károlyi decided to carry out a moderate land reform which included compensation of former owners, this issue divided the Socialist party. The right wing, which was numerically smaller but more influential and better represented in the government, supported Károlyi, but the rest of the party demanded the socialization of large estates. Before the reform could be carried out, the Károlyi regime collapsed and the right wing was excluded from the Social party.[22]

The Communists were not devided over this issue: both Kun and Szamuely rejected Lenin's tactics of winning the peasants by concessions. They believed Hungary to be more advanced than Russia and therefore imagined that in their

---

garian Proletarian Dictatorship), (Ekaterinburg: Tsentral'noi Biuro Vengerskoi Sektsii pri Ts. K.R.K.P. (b), 1920).

[22] On Communist and Socialist agrarian policies see Vera Szemere, *Az Agrárkérdés 1918–1919–ben* (The Agrarian Question in 1918–1919), (Budapest: Kossuth, 1963).

country it would be possible to introduce Socialist agriculture immediately. The Communist program, on whose basis the unification took place, demanded a "determined struggle aganist land reform" and envisaged even the co-operatives as merely temporary institutions, useful until everything became state property. The Socialists, as well as the Communists, liked this solution, which combined radicalism in theory with inaction in practice.

The differences of opinion on agricultural policy were not between Communists and Socialists, but between the representatives of the two urban parties and the agrarian radicals.[23] The agrarian radical movement had a long history in Hungary, but because of police terror and the prejudices of Socialist leaders it grew up in isolation from the Socialist party. Following defeat in World War I, a wave of peasant disturbances occurred, and when the Soviet Republic was founded the Marxist leaders made an effort to integrate the representatives of the radical peasants into the new regime. The Commissariat for Agriculture was headed by a "college" made up of three Socialists, one Communist, and Sándor Csizmadia, who had long played a role in the peasant movements, even though he belonged to the Socialist party. However, the old differences and distrust between the representatives of urban and rural revolutionary movements did not disappear. Agrarian Socialist leaders did not win as many positions in the regime as they felt they deserved and even Csizmadia himself was soon forced out.

The Soviet regime accomplished practically nothing in the villages: the small holders and owners of medium-size estates were allowed to keep their holdings, and only the large estates were nationalized. But this was only nation-

---

[23] This point is made forcefully in Chapter III.

alization in words, because the regime needed experts to continue production, and the new managers could only have been the old owners and bailiffs. The Commissariat of Agriculture was interested in assuring production rather than in satisfying the demands of the peasants. Consequently, they wanted to prevent changes which would be disruptive. The peasantry was bitterly disappointed.

This disappointment came to the surface on the occasion of the meeting of the National Congress of Councils in June 1919. The policies of the regime met with ferocious criticism from rural delegates, who denounced what they regarded as an insufficient reorganization of village life, and also attacked such central features of the regime, as bureaucratization and centralization. In general, they exhibited hostility to an urban way of life. In response to their criticism, the Communist and Socialist members of the government took an identical position.[24]

The short-sighted agricultural policy undoubtedly contributed to the fall of the regime. Although a land reform could not have saved the Soviet government, it would have made much more difficult the conservative reconstruction carried out in the Horthy period. Foreign policy was a far more crucial issue for the survival of the Republic. Unlike land reform, foreign policy stirred a passionate debate within the ruling party, and in this debate we find Communists and Socialists on both sides.

It is an irony in the history of the Soviet Republic that the only party which had not only eschewed nationalism, but had proudly declared itself to be internationalist, came to power in order to defend the integrity of the fatherland. Whatever had been their previous ideologies

---

[24] A *tanácsok országos gyülésének naplója (Records of the National Congress of Councils)*, (Budapest: Atheneum, 1919). See especially the records for the days June 17 and 21.

and slogans, the Communists proved themselves to be better patriots than the "nationalist" Right, which in the crucial hours conspired with foreign enemies, who had the announced intention of dismembering the country.

Socialists and Communists shared basic assumptions about foreign policy. They agreed that the republic should base its policy on the expectation of world revolution and Russian help. This is a point which hardly needs proof, for had the Socialists and different ideas, they would never have invited the Communists to participate in the government. The Socialists believed that this policy could be carried out only with Communist help. This was why the only commissariat headed by a Communist was that for foreign affairs.

In the perspective of time it is clear that these two assumptions were incorrect, and this error was the reason for the fall of the regime. However, it would be wrong to blame the leaders for a lack of realism. The expectation of world revolution was widely held—and not only in Hungary—by people whose realism is generally beyond dispute—Lenin, for example. Nor was the expectation of Russian help naive. The Bolsheviks had every intention of interfering.[25] Their inability to do so was caused by the fortunes of the Russian Civil War, which no one in Hungary could have predicted. But above all, assuming that the goal of keeping Hungarians under Hungarian authority was a valid one, it is hard to see on what other

[25] The plans for invading Rumania and thereby establishing contact with Hungary had already been drawn up in Moscow. They were not realized partly because of the successes of the Whites under General A. I. Denikin and partly because of the defection of Ataman G. Gregorev from the Red Army. Arthur E. Adams, *Bolsheviks in the Ukraine: The Second Campaign 1918–1919* (New Haven: Yale University Press, 1963), pp. 238–241.

basis the regime could have formed its policy. The expectation of Russian help was more realistic than was the expectation of the goodwill and wisdom of the *Entente.*

There could be no debate about the basic orientation of foreign policy but there were disagreements about implementation. The question was: how ready should the country be to make concessions to the enemy in the hope of finding accommodation?

The Soviet Republic had two opportunities to find a compromise with the *Entente*: On April 4 General Smuts came to Budapest, offering somewhat better terms than the ones included in the Vyx note, which had brought down the Károlyi regime. Two Communists, Elek Bolgár and Béla Kun, and two Socialists, Sándor Garbai and Zsigmond Kunfi, negotiated with the general.[26] Kun recommended to his colleagues the rejection of the offer. He argued that a Brest-Litovsk type peace would destroy the regime, which came to power on the basis of nationalism, and that this peace might endanger the Soviet alliance.[27] His position was adopted by the Governing Council.

The second opportunity came in the middle of June, when Clemenceau demanded the evacuation of newly occupied territories and promised in exchange that the Rumanians would retire to a previously agreed line. The government received Clemenceau's note at the time when the First Congress of Soviets was meeting in Budapest. The question how the country should respond to this note gave rise to the most serious debate in the history of the republic.[28]

---

[26] On Smuts mission see Harold Nicholson, *Peacemaking 1919* (New York: Universal Library, 1965), pp. 292–308.

[27] Böhm, *op. cit.,* pp. 280–285.

[28] For the debate see *A tanácsok országos gyülésének naplója* (Records of the National Congress of Councils), June 19.

The course of the debate is extremely instructive, for one can see how, under the guise of different phraseology, politicians of different backgrounds were arguing for the same policy. Kun, perhaps under the impact of developments in Russia, or because of his understanding of the weakness of the Hungarian army, reversed his April decision and now argued for concessions. He was supported by one of the most influential Socialists, Kunfi, who avoided Kun's talk about world revolution and stated frankly that the people wanted peace and that the Hungarians should care above all for the interests of their own revolution. Kunfi, with conscious irony, prefaced his remarks: "No matter how unpleasant and perhaps compromising it is for Comrade Kun, I must say that I consider his general remarks about our foreign policy correct."[79] Kun's policy was attacked by Communists and Socialists. The socialist József Pogány talked about military necessity, and how the army must not give up railroad centers, whereas Samuely, like a segment of the Russian left-wing Communists, argued that there could be no negotiations with the imperialists.

It was Kun's policy which prevailed. However, concessions could not save the regime: a few weeks later, when it became obvious that the Rumanian troops could not be stopped, the commissars went into exile.

In conclusion we should pose the question which was merely implied in this chapter, namely: What was the relation of forces within the coalition? I have tried to make it clear that it is not helpful to compare the role of the two parties, because old party labels had lost most of their meaning. Instead, one must examine the influence of individual leaders, or perhaps the influence of groups within

---

[29] *Ibid.*, p. 18.

the government. But if one must designate the senior partner of the two participating parties, it seems preferable to name the Socialists.

The majority of the workers remained loyal to their trusted leaders. Unification and the experience of the Soviet Republic did not radicalize the proletariat and participation in the government took away from the Communists the powerful weapon of being in opposition. Under the circumstances, there could be no question of former Communists taking over trade-union or party organizations in which Socialist leaders were entrenched by seniority. Communist weakness was proved over and over again. The Budapest Council of Workers' and Soldiers' Deputies, elected in April, was dominated by Socialists; its 80-man Executive Committee contained only twenty-four Communists, and its 5-man Presidium only one.[30] The weakness of the Communists was even more conclusively demonstrated at the First Congress of the United Party in June, when they could count on only 60-90 delegates out of 327. They suffered the most humiliating defeat on the election of the Executive Committee. The Congress refused to elect Communists (with the exception of Kun), and only when Kun and his old comrades threatened to break up the party did the Socialist leaders succeed in persuading the delegates to accept the original list which contained four Communists out of thirteen.[31] (The Congress, however, accepted a purely Communist program without debate, proving once again that the differences were personal, rather than ideological.) The debate surrounding the composition of the Executive Committee revealed the extent of the Com-

[30] Rudolf, L. Tökés, *Bela Kun and the Hungarian Soviet Republic* (New York: Praeger, 1967), p. 161.
[31] *Ibid.*, pp. 176–184.

munists weakness and the nature of their strength.[32] Communists and Socialists needed each other equally, for once the coalition was formed any rupture in it would have opened the way to counterrevolution.

It is hard to speculate on what would have happened to the coalition had the regime survived longer. The differences between radical and totalitarian mentality on the one hand, and the democratic and liberal perspective on the other, would probably have come to the surface. Quite possibly, Communist and Socialist parties might have reemerged with a membership different than they had had before the merger. But the awareness of latent differences should not obscure the fact that the cooperation, for a limited period and for limited purposes, did work.

Communists and Socialists, at least temporarily, had undergone a profound change: they came to identify with their new roles as revolutionary statesmen. The Socialists found it thrilling to regard themselves in the vanguard of world revolution, and to act according to ideas which they had preached but only half believed all their lives. The Communists, too, who had scorned the idea of national independence, now measured their personal success in terms of the national interests of Hungary. The Socialists and the Communists in the government had wanted to remain in power and to save their regime but had only a limited range of options. In this limited range, there was no room for ideological disagreements.

---

[32] See the Party program in *A Magyar munkásmozgalom történetének válogatott dokumentumai (Selected Documents of the History of the Hungarian Workers' Movement)* VI, Part B (Budapest: Kossuth, 1960), 49–53.

3

The Agrarian Opposition at the National Congress of Councils

Andrew C. Janos

BY THE general agreement of contemporaries and the students of the period the revolutions of 1918–1919 represented the rising tide of urban politics against an old regime whose roots were deeply embedded in the traditions and values of rural Hungary. Budapest, therefore, the only truly metropolitan center in the country, was extolled by the Left as the "heart of the revolution" and, conversely, denounced by the Right after the victory of the counter-revolution in November 1919 as the "sinful city."

Accordingly, the principal political cleavage of Hungarian society during the turbulent year of the revolutions ran between the city and the countryside. For although Budapest was the center of the great political upheaval, the provinces surrounding it gave succor and comfort to the defenders of the old regime. As early as December 1918 the banner of the counterrevolution was raised in Catholic Transdanubia, the Hungarian Vendée, where a number of conservative landowners and church men vowed to lead a Christian and nationalist crusade against the godless and treacherous capital. At that time the expected conservative groundswell did not materialize, but its threat was real enough to cause the indefinite postponement of parliamentary elections by the embattled Károlyi regime. The democratic republic was then toppled by the Left and not by the Right ushering in the Soviet Republic and increasing the wariness of rural Hungary. Motivated by a proprietary instinct and bolstered by the continued influence of the Church and the traditional elites in the villages, peasant smallholders and sharecroppers refused to cooperate with the new regime, were reluctant to deliver food for the city, and in general sabotaged the economic measures of the the Soviet government. When the latter attempted to enforce its policies, scores of villages rose in arms against the proletarian dictatorship.

This aspect of the revolution is well-known and amply documented by historians and contemporaries whether they represented the viewpoint of the left or the right. Indeed, for most observers, the "agrarian problem" held significant lessons to be incorporated in their divergent doctrines of politics. For the Left the experience served as a further proof that the peasantry was a backward social class that might be manipulated, perhaps bribed into compliance, but never trusted as a true revolutionary ally. For the Right, the lesson was that the peasantry was the only genuinely Hungarian class and the carrier of the values of the nation, themes that were to become the leitmotifs for the populist and national radical ideologies of the interwar years.

In drawing these politically significant conclusions, however, the protagonists of both Left and Right overlooked the fact that the agrarian problem had another dimension and that, apart from the conservative opposition of the peasantry, a second agrarian opposition existed that drew its inspiration not from religion, tradition, and proprietary instinct but from chiliastic and anarchistic ideas common among rebels in primitive societies. The second opposition, like the first, resented the rise and preponderance of the city in politics but, unlike the conservatives, combined its resistance to modernity and industrial socialism with a Messianic quest for a communal and egalitarian society. In this spirit, the second agrarian opposition attacked the urban revolution not from the Right but from the Left condemning it not for subverting the traditional order of society but for not being radical and consistent enough in the pursuit of this objective.

The origins of this agrarian radicalism went back to the 1890's when many rural areas of eastern Europe experienced social unrest following the advances of a money economy and the rapid disintegration of traditional society, two processes that also coincided with a prolonged and continent-wide agricultural depression. As was pointed out in Chapter I, in Hungary this unrest was most intensive in the Stormy Corner, an economically highly developed region of the country where the influence of large estates was limited but where the relatively prosperous smallholding peasantry coexisted uneasily with a large semi-employed agricultural proletariat. The Social Democratic party made several attempts to enlist the support of these agrarian laborers only to be frustrated by police measures and the innate distrust of the rural proletariat toward urban leaders and political organization. Thus throughout the years that led to World War I the agrarian Socialist movement maintained a separate identity and remained almost exclusively under the leadership of local elites drawn from the socially marginal element of the Hungarian countryside. In 1901, for instance, the twenty-eight agrarian Socialists who ran unsuccessfully for parliament included six shoemakers, two masons, two blacksmiths, two carpenters, two farmhands, two hawkers, two mechanics, two journalists, one trader, and seven whose occupations are unknown.[1] Most prominent among these candidates was Sándor Csizmadia, a self-educated journalist and peasant poet, Zoltán Várkonyi, a former horsetrader *(kupec)*, and Vilmos Mezöffi, a provincial journalist. Mezöffi and another agrarian radical, András Achim, were eventually elected to the House of Representatives, the first Socialists ever to sit in that body.

The agrarian Socialist movement reached its height in the middle of the first decade of the century. Thereafter it gradually declined under the dual impact of police repression and a slow improvement in economic conditions. During World War I the agrarian Socialists were inactive. However, upon the collapse of the old regime they rapidly reemerged from their passivity. In the winter of 1918–1919 agrarian Socialists led the rural proletariat against manors and provincial administrative centers—and, in the first days of March 1919, appropriated landholdings. In the country of Somogy they even succeeded in seizing power and proclaimed the dictatorship of the proletariat two weeks before similar events took place in Budapest. Meanwhile the half-defunct Association of Agrarian Laborers was revitalized, and its membership increased spectacularly (from 1,300 in 1917 to 40,000 by the end of 1918 and 580,000 by spring 1919).[2]

These activities made the agrarian Socialists natural

---

[1] Zoltan Bodrogközy, *A magyar agrármozgalmak története* (History of Hungarian Agrarian Movements), (Budapest: Légrády, 1929), p. 77.
[2] Albert Király, *Zwei Jahre Arbeiterbewegung in Ungarn* (Wien, 1922), p. 17.

allies of the Communist party, and when the Soviet Republic was proclaimed they were coopted into the regime to fill in the vacuum left by the collapse of the old system of public administration. The agrarian Socialists were thus selected to occupy seats on provinicial councils and their executive committees, the so-called directories. However, the old suspicions of the rural revolutionary movement persisted and when it came to the higher posts of the party and the Revolutionary Governing Council, their representatives were bypassed. Csizmadia was invited to become commissar for agriculture but even he was to exercise his powers jointly within a "college" consisting of five members. In turn, the agrarian revolutionaries continued to guard jealously the organizational independence of the Association of Agricultural Laborers and turned it into an instrument of resisting the policies of the central authorities. Not surprisingly therefore the role of the association became the source of both conflict and recriminations between urban and rural socialists and the main reason for Csizmadia's early removal from the Agricultural College of the Revolutionary Governing Council.

An institutional context to the conflict between agrarian and industrial Socialists was provided by the Soviet constitution promulgated a few days after the proclamation of the republic. In accordance with these provisions local councils were elected throughout the nation on April 7, 1919. Balloting was on a single list and, even though the dictatorship was only two weeks old at the time, the monopoly of the list was effectively enforced. (An opposition list appeared in one constituency only, the Eighth District of Budapest, and won over the official list, but the results were quickly annulled and new elections were held with an outcome that was satisfactory to the government.)[3] Through this device the dictatorship eliminated all conservative, "bourgeois," or right-wing Socialist opposition. On the other hand, the Revolutionary Governing Council, itself divided, had no power to impose monolithic unity and the system of councils that emerged continued to reflect divisions within the revolutionary camp itself—and, despite repeated efforts to centralize administration, maintained considerable independence from the Soviet government in Budapest.

In terms of constitutional provisions these councils were to elect the National Congress of Councils, the supreme legislative organ of the Soviet Republic. The articles under which these elections took place were designed to favor the capital and discriminate against the countryside. These discriminatory provisions were coupled by considerable pressures applied by the central government, but even so, under the chaotic conditions of warfare and counterrevolutionary risings, a sufficient number of councils defied the central authorities to send independent-minded delegates to the Soviet parliament. Among them were about seventy delegates who formed the hard core of what was to become an agrarian or "provincial" opposition against the majority of industrial Socialists at the Congress.

The presence of this opposition was immediately obvious when the 348 members of the Congress convened on June 14, 1919.[4] Hardly did the festive opening speeches end when one of the provincial delegates rose to welcome "this first opportunity since March to tell in public what

[3] See Vilmos Böhm, *Két forradalom tüzében* (In the Crossfire of Two Revolutions), (Wien: Bécsi magyar Kiadó, 1923, pp. 300–301.

[4] It was characteristic of the prevailing confusion that 413 delegates had showed up at the Congress but only 348 were found to have valid credentials. Another 30 delegates were later added when members of the National Economic Council were coopted.

is in our minds,"[5] and a colleague of his spoke of the need
to end the "dictatorship exercised against the proletariat"
by the Revolutionary Governing Council. The same delegate reminded the people's commissars pointedly that the
Congress was an "autonomous body" whose decisions would
bind the government.[6]

The provincial opposition scored an early success
when the Congress accepted liberal rules of procedure that
placed no limitation on the number and length of speeches.
Then, for two days, the delegates listened to reports from
People's Commissars Erdélyi, Lengyel, Nyisztor, Hamburger, and the later famous economist Eugene (Jenö)
Varga, interrupted only by impatient exclamations and
occasional jeers. But when the reports had been delivered,
relatively unknown provincial delegates took the floor with
a torrent of complaints and violent abuse.

On June 18, the fifth consecutive day of turbulent
debate, the provincials and the urban delegates (as they
now habitually referred to each other) faced their first
parliamentary test of strength. The Committee on Credentials presented a motion to seat thirty representatives
of the National Economic Council, in effect appointed by
the government. After a brief but acrimonious debate the
motion was put to vote and carried by 100 votes against 78.[7]

The next day the provincials surprised the Congress
by submitting an emergency draft resolution to the effect
that a commission of twelve should be appointed, with half
of its members selected from the provincial delegates, to

[5] *A Tanácsok Országos Gyülésének Naplója, 1919 junius 14—1919
junius 23* (Records of the National Congress of Councils) (Budapest:
Athenaeum, 1919), from here cited as *T.O.G.* See the speech of Jozsef
Schneff, June 15, No. 2, p. 4.

[6] *T.O.G.*, June 15, No. 2, p. 6.

[7] For the debate and vote see *ibid.*, June 18, No. 5, pp. 1–7.

investigate malpractices in the people's commissariats.[8]
After another brief debate this motion was rejected by a
voice vote on the ground that such commission would
usurp the functions of the plenary sessions of the Congress.
A few hours later the government retaliated by requesting
a change in the rules of procedure to allow the presiding
officer of the Congress to impost cloture on the stormy
economic debate and a time limit of ten minutes on every
speech save for the reports of people's commissars. The
motion was carried and the limitations imposed, despite
the fact that 43 more delegates had signed up to speak to
the economic reports alone.[9] "The voice of the province
has been muffled," exclaimed an angry delegate, according
to the testimony of the transcripts.[10] On the next two days
the provincials were subjected to insults and had to listen
to charges of "immaturity," "chicanery," and counterrevolutionary activity. As the sessions dragged through the
lame debate of the draft constitution there were irritated
demands to end the "blabbing contest" and the waste of
precious time.

Finally, in what was tantamount to a parliamentary
coup d'état, the motion was made to adjourn the plenary
sessions and delegate the powers of the Congress to a standing committee. If anyone had doubts about the purpose
of this motion they were dispelled by the election and the
composition of the committee. The 150 members to exercise
the powers of the Congress were not elected individually or
by proportional representation but on a single list submitted by a nominating committee. This system enabled the
majority to eliminate the members of the provincial opposi-

---

[8] *Ibid.,* June 20, No. 7, p. 13.

[9] *Ibid.,* June 20, No. 7, p. 22.

[10] *Ibid.,* June 20, No. 7, p. 22.

tion. In its final form the list included 102 delegates from Budapest, 40 from provincial cities, and only 8 from rural areas. The provincials put up a list of their own but the official slate won easily with 158 against 43 votes. Though the Soviet government had a clear majority at the Congress, it is obvious from the transcripts that the vote was taken at a moment when many provincial delegates were absent from the session.

The provincials were thus silenced and reviled, and there is little doubt that the opposition, together with the Association of Agricultural Laborers, were already marked for liquidation. As it happened, however, the provincial cadres were not liquidated by their fellow revolutionaries, but by the armed detachments of the counterrevolution. While the majority of the urban leaders succeeded in escaping to Austria after the fall of the Republic, the rural revolutionaries stayed on and fell victims of punitive expeditions that sought them out with special ferocity as targets of their revenge.

The first target of the attacks of the agrarians was the "new bureaucracy," the system of political and production commissars that the government created in order to subdue the refractory councils and to mobilize the meager resources of the provinces. But apart from these immediate political threats, bureaucracy also raised a broader ideological concern that it would not only subvert the proletarian state of self-governing communes, but also the idea of an egalitarian society by providing a source of social status and privilege.

"I cannot easily comprehend these foreign sounding words," said the delegate Topa amidst slight amusement in the hall, "but I gather that proletarian bureaucracy is

just another term for a new privileged class. (Approval.)
It appears to me that in the general turbulence of the
proletarian revolution certain people were thrown to the
surface whose only title to fame is that they spent some
time in Russian prisoner-of-war camps where, frankly,
they had shown themselves incapable of absorbing as
much as a penny's worth of true revolutionary experience."[11]

Many complaints voiced by the provincials sound familiar.
They are as old as the conflict of incomprehension between
the industrial city and the agrarian countryside. The man
of cities, they repeated endlessly, clever as he might be, had
no understanding for the subtleties of the agrarian
economy and society. Thus one István Tóth from Transdanubia lamented:

On the black wings of nepotism and bureaucracy the production commissars fly out into the countryside, but their
knowledge of farming has been acquired from illustrated
books of tales. There was a commissar in the Enying
district who suggested that we sow wheat in April.
(Laughter.) [12]

An even more serious complaint was that the urban
"bureaucrat" or "commissar" did not "speak the language"
or understand the thinking of the rural population. Therefore, the bureaucrat from the Center was likely to stir
up trouble and then let the local council face up to the
consequences. The provincials particularly resented the
antireligious agitation of young Communist zealots from
Budapest. Their complaints were summed up by the articu-
late Lajos Jankovits who during the first sessions had

[12] *Ibid.*, June 17, No. 4, p. 20.
[12] *Ibid.*, June 17, No. 4, p. 20.

emerged as one of the chief spokesmen of the agrarian opposition:

> These agitators have caused immense trouble and harm in the villages. The directories in the countryside performed their work well, quietly and in a disciplined manner. We could have continued like that except for the political commissioners who began to swarm all over the country like a cloud of locusts. They descended upon the villages and began their work by declaring that the churches would be converted into movie houses. (Exclamations: Leave us alone! Let the councils work in peace!) [13]

The attacks on the bureaucracy were not only expressed in political and administrative but also in racial terms. These attacks, invited by the presence of Jewish commissars on the Revolutionary Governing Council,[14] were demagogic and motivated by a tactical opportunism but, at the same time, they also had certain ideological underpinnings. Anti-Semitism was not entirely alien to the syndicalist theories in which the agrarian Socialists had been nurtured, and Marx himself, as is well-known, in his early writings had described Jews as the prime agents of capitalism.[15] Inspired by these sources the agrarians at the

---

[13] *Ibid.*, June 17, No. 4, p. 26.

[14] The membership of the Revolutionary Council varied between 29 and 34 people's commissars and deputy commissars. However, altogether, 45 persons served in the council during the 133 days of the Soviet Republic of whom, in the accounts of various authors, 30 to 34 were Jewish or "of Jewish origin." For these figures and for a variety of estimates on the composition of the council I am indebted to William O. McCagg, "Hungary's Jewish Ministers and Commissars," paper presented at the Berkeley Conference on the Hungarian Soviet Republic.

[15] Karl Marx, "The Jewish Question," also, "The Capacity of Today's Jews and Christians to Be Free." For the text of these essays see Dago-

Congress made a habit of using "capitalist" and "Jew" interchangeably insidiously insisting that, in the guise of commissars, members of the former exploiting classes had infiltrated the proletarian state. The fact that most Jewish commissars were intellectuals of midde-class background seemed only to corroborate the thesis and lent force to the argument.

The anti-Semitism of the agrarians was manifested in subtle references to nepotism, religion, and social background as well as in the form of open attacks. Gyula Vojticzky of the county of Heves denounced irresponsible commissars "whatever their religious affiliation may have been."[16] The blacksmith Topa made sarcastic remarks about the composition of the Kun government,[17] while Sándor Iványi implied that Jews, for reasons of economic interest, were natural counterrevolutionaries.[18] Jenö Varga's speech touched off a minor demonstration on the floor with shouts of "get out the Jews!"[19] and there is sufficient evidence that a number of blatantly anti-Semitic speeches were later expunged from the transcript. The anti-Semitic mood and the slogans emerge unmistakably from Béla Kun's angry rebuttal:

> What is happening behind the front line, indeed at this very Congress, is open incitement for pogrom and counter-revolution. It happened here in this very hall yesterday that a hand-written pogrom leaflet was circulated and then smuggled on the table of one of our comrades. . . . How can

---

bert D. Runes, ed., *A World Without Jews* (New York: Philosophical Library, 1960).

[16] *T.O.G.*, June 20, No. 7, p. 10.

[17] *Ibid.*, June 17, No. 4, p. 17.

[18] *Ibid.*, June 21, No. 8, p. 9.

[19] *Ibid.*, June 16, No. 3, p. 6.

the Red Army fight and maintain its morale when at this National Congress of Councils, and even at the party congress people agitate against the Jews and instigate pogroms?

The peasants starve out the city and revolt. The province is in the flames of the counterrevolution not only, to quote Comrade Horváth,[20] because the place is swarming all over with *bochers* (Exclamation by Bêla Vágo: "And people with earlocks"), but mainly because the provincial comrades show no willingness to make any sacrifice. . . . A Jew as I am, I am not embarrassed to raise these issues. My father was a Jew but I am no longer one, for I became a Socialist and a Communist. But many others who were born in the Christian religion remained what they were: Christian Socialists.[21]

The provincial delegates were also outraged by the agricultural policies of the Soviet Republic. The regime had socialized the large estates—a measure that dogmatic agrarian Socialists could not but welcome—but it had spared the holdings of the rich peasantry and thereby preserved the material foundations of the traditional structure of rural society. Then, as if to add insult to injury, the bailiffs and "agronomists" of the estates—the hated symbols of the overthrown social order—had been retained to manage socialized farms in order to assure the continuity of production and public supply. In the words of Jenö Hamburger, one of the members of the agricultural college:

There are some agronomists who long for the restoration of the capitalist order, yet I must emphatically declare

---

[20] This speech was apparently deleted from the record.
[21] *T.O.G.*, June 21, No. 8, p. 22.

that without them Budapest would today face the prospect of starvation.[22]

As to peasant smallholders, Hamburger explained:

> One of the major obstacles in the way of socializing all land is the consideration we must give to the protection of this year's harvest. Any measure that would adversely affect the crop would expose the urban proletariat and the army to famine. This we will have to prevent at any cost.[23]

Another member of the college, György Nyisztor, echoed Hamburger's words as if to underline their importance. The proletarian dictatorship took the side of the expert against the revolutionary and argued in terms of expediency over ideology:

> Strong criticism has been voiced here concerning our agricultural experts. We are not going to defend them from their critics. Yet at the same time we must declare with the same decisiveness that socialist production is absolutely impossible without skilled technicians in agriculture. (Noise.) Ten, twenty, or a hundred acres may be cultivated without technical expertise, but not estates of a thousand, ten thousand, or a hundred thousand acres. I grant you, that bailiff stood there only yesterday with a whip in his hand as his master's slave driver. His soul had been soaked in bourgeois ideology. But for heaven's sake, tell me where on earth could we find suitable, skilled substitutes? [24]

The provincials were hardly impressed by these pleas. Theirs was a revolution against the large estates, the bailiffs,

22 *Ibid.*, June 17, No. 4, p. 5.
23 *Ibid.*, June 17, No. 4, p. 9.
24 *Ibid.*, June 20, No. 7, p. 13.

and the rich peasantry whom one of their numbers described as "those leeches, bloodsuckers, snakes . . . the worst
and most ferocious enemies of the Soviet Republic."[25] If the
people's commissars wanted to act pragmatic they should do
so at the expense of the industrial and not the agricultural
proletariat and spare the urban capitalists from expropri-
ation. This issue dominated every provincial speech and
their repetitiousness utterly exasperated the urban delegates, as one can see in the following exchange.

Lajos Jankovits:

> Finally, I want to return to statements concerning the agri-
> cultural experts. Unfortunately, the old owners and their
> bailiffs remain at the estates and their behavior shows
> precious little change. The Revolutionary Governing
> Council committed a serious mistake when it believed in
> their declarations of loyalty.

György Nyisztor, people's commissar:

> We did not believe them. We simply needed trained men.

Lajos Jankovits:

> Domestic servants gave declarations of confidence and this
> was regarded as adequate proof to appoint Count Janko-
> vits [26] production manager on his own land.

György Nyisztor:

> We needed a qualified and trained individual!

Lajos Jankovits:

---

[25] Sándor Kovács, *Ibid.*, June 18, No. 5, p. 34.
[26] No relation to the speaker.

The count never performed any productive labor. His servants, bailiffs and agronomists did the work.

György Nyisztor:

Enough of this rubbish! You cannot cultivate 20,000 acres without some expertise.[27]

These arguments over "redness and expertise" may have sounded even more futile because most of the provincials showed little appreciation for the technical and organizational complexities of a modern economic system and society. Theirs was a happy, rustic and basically voluntaristic world of virtue in which obstacles could be overcome by will. Some of the speeches at the Congress are reminiscent of the raw economic primitivism of contemporary Chinese communism pinpointing some of the fundamental differences between the urban and the rural revolution in the modern age. The following is an excerpt from the answer of a speaker to an interjection that short of technical improvements the mines would have to close down and this would produce a crisis in the supply of fuel:

So what! If the coal mines close down we still have our forests. Most of our forests have not been cut for the last few years. If we don't have coal we will run the engines and locomotives on wood! (Exclamations: "Nonsense! You can't use wood for that!" Great noise. President rings bell.) Don't you worry! I can make fire with wood, and if I have no coal I am not embarrassed to use it. . . . As to the loss of iron mines, there is plenty of ore underground. The proletarians will dig at it and get it.[28]

---

27 *Ibid.*, June 17, No. 4, p. 27.
28 *Ibid.*, June 20, No. 7, p. 2.

Similarly, the delegate Topa proposed to solve the problem of food shortages in the capital by urging the industrial workers to travel to the outskirts and grow vegetables on the patches of land they might find on their way:

> They [the urban population] should take their streetcars and travel to the outskirts and try to grow a few heads of cabbage. No, they do not do this because they are worried about calluses on their hands. They are afraid of the sight of soil. They do not want to grow cabbages or carrots. They would rather linger on the streets and wail: give us food because we are starving! Let us go to work, comrades! Give a few hours to the tilling of the soil instead of listening to concerts.[29]

Topa's remarks gave an indication of the hostility of the peasants not only toward the organization men of the bureaucracy but also toward the industrial proletariat. The "objective cause" of this hostility, as a Marxist observer would say, was the problem of allocating scant resources among the urban and the rural population both of which expected the revolution to fulfill pent-up economic expectations overnight. This is to say that some conflict along economic class lines was inevitable under prevailing conditions. Yet it is also certain that several "subjective" factors had contributed to exacerbate the frustrations of the agricultural proletariat. Most significantly, the economic policies of the Soviet Republic, as the provincials bitterly charged, had been designed to bribe the industrial proletariat into compliance at the expense of the agrarian population. In the factories the government had introduced the eight-hour day while in agriculture it retained the twelve-to-fourteen hour routine. The Revolutionary Governing Council had also

---

[29] *Ibid.*, June 17, No. 4, p. 17.

maintained differential wage rates in industry and agriculture and pursued fiscal policies that favored the city over the countryside. The authorities enforced rigidly the circulation of the inflated Soviet banknotes in the villages, but not in the cities, which meant that the peasant was forced to sell his food reserves for money that did not buy him much needed industrial articles or, for that matter, anything else. These policies had been motivated as much by ideology as by political expediency. The urban Socialists regarded the workers as a class with an historical mission and they were reinforced in their beliefs by the sustained support they received from the industrial proletariat.

These justifications made little sense to the peasants. What was obvious and reasonable to the urban intellectuals who led the Soviet Republic represented a gross breach of the egalitarian faith to the peasant radical. Topa stated curtly:

> It cannot be our intent in this proletarian state to let one group subsist on the sweat and toil of the agricultural population, thus elevating the industrial proletariat to the position of a ruling class. Therefore I ask you, comrades, to improve the lot of the agricultural worker. . . . The man of the scythe needs better wages.[30]

The statements of the urban Communist that the agricultural proletariat had lifted no finger in the class struggle and that the villages were liberated by the industrial proletariat were indignantly rejected. The delegate Lajos Urbán said:

> I must tell you comrades, that the agricultural workers have the right to call themselves the vanguard inasmuch as

---

[30] *Ibid.,* June 17, No. 4, p. 14.

they were the first revolutionaries in Hungary at the time of György Dózsa.[31] (Approval and Applause.) Therefore, comrades, we cannot allow the industrial proletariat to voice even the slightest recriminations against the poor peasantry. I cannot allow this because the agricultural proletariat joined us with enthusiasm when the first sounds of the revolution had reached us. When we began to lay the foundations of this Republic of Councils they all listened to what we had to say and became enthusiastic communists. They as well as their leaders are beyond reproach. They are not counterrevolutionaries by any stretch of the imagination. Such charges are unfounded. The agricultural proletariat was the first one to plough the wild earth and prepare the soil for the seeds of communism.[32]

Other delegates were not content merely to defend their constituents. They returned urban reproaches with interest and accused the industrial workers of undermining revolutionary morale. If the agricultural workers acted in "such despicable manner" as described by some of the people's commissars this was only because they had been corrupted by an "idle and loud-mouthed" urban proletariat.[33] Another delegate charged that the workers in the factories failed to fulfill their revolutionary obligations; to support his argument, he contrasted sagging industrial production with the continued efficiency of farming. The problem was not the shortage of strategic raw materials but simply the laziness of factory workers.[34] In general, the provincial delegates compared the softness of the city with the sturdiness of peasant life and strongly implied that the urban classes

---

[31] Leader of the great peasant rebellion of 1514.

[32] *Ibid.,* June 17, No. 4, p. 26.

[33] *Ibid.,* June 17, No. 4, p. 13.

[34] Vojticzky, *Ibid.,* June 22, No. 7, p. 8.

were too decadent to play a leading role in the revolution. The urban workers, said the self-righteous Topa, were "accustomed to concerts and God-knows-what other sedentary amusements."[35] Others expressed their contempt for those who rode streetcars or walked on nicely paved streets. The critique that poured forward was obviously overdrawn, even grotesque, in view of conditions prevailing in Budapest and of the generally low economic and cultural standards of the Hungarian working class. But then one has to remember that rural living standards were still far below the urban level. There was a pathetic element in this class struggle between the more and the most impoverished. But it was class struggle nonetheless fought in terms of the primordial egalitarianism of the agrarian Socialist. At least one of these speeches deserves quoting in some detail:

> I observe here in the capital that people promenade in fashionable clothes. I have not seen one to walk around barefoot. At the same time the farm folk are unable to cover their naked bodies because a full day's, nay a week's wage, is not enough to buy a patch over their rags. Contradictions. Voice: "Go to the Angyalföld,[36] you can see them there!" Noise. "Hear! Hear!" President rings bell.) The people here in the city ride comfortably in their street-cars and saunter on paved streets! . . . Even the best of the Socialists becomes a counterrevolutionary overnight when he sees the class differences that still exist today. (Approval.) When agricultural workers see the mademoiselles and their gigolos prance on the streets all day they are likely to make a few unprintable remarks. When all this is here for the eye to see, it is unnecessary to inquire any further why the farm workers are boiling with rage and

---

[35] *Ibid.*, June 17, No. 4, p. 13.
[36] One of the poorest of the industrial outskirts of Budapest.

why they will eventually explode. But when the explosion
occurs there will be trouble here! [37]

The fall of the Soviet Republic and the decimation of
the provincial Communists was not the last chapter in the
history of Hungarian rural radicalism. True, for more than
a decade after 1919 there was silence in the Hungarian countryside, enforced by police measures, and sustained by a
moderate economic upswing in the mid-twenties. But at the
time of the world crisis chiliastic agrarianism reappeared, in
keeping with the times, under fascist labels. In 1931 the so-
called Scythe Cross was founded by a certain Zoltán Böszörmény and drew considerable following in the former strongholds of the agrarian Socialist movements. Despite the fascist label, the character and leadership of agrarian radicalism changed little. The most notable feat of the Scythe Cross
was a naïve attempt to seize political power in the country.
On May 1, 1936, several thousands of its members gathered
in the village of Dévaványa and prepared to march against
Budapest under the slogan "Kill the lords and the Jews."
The authorities put down the rebellion with ease and 700
peasants were arrested, 113 tried and 87 sentenced to imprisonment. Böszörmény escaped to Germany whence he
reemerged only in 1945 to petition the triumphant Communist party for membership.[38] More than anything else,
this request symbolized the revolutionary character and, at
the same time, the homelessness of chiliastic agrarianism in
the modern political spectrum.

Böszörmény's request was turned down and the Com-

[37] Ferenc Vogel, *ibid.*, June 18, No. 5, pp. 11–12.
[38] For an English language source, see C. A. Macartney, *October Fifteenth, A History of Modern Hungary, 1929–1945* (Edinburgh: The
University Press, 1967), 2nd ed., pp. 157–159.

munist party treated the problem of agrarian radicalism with utmost caution. Instead of capturing the revolutionary potential of the rural proletarian masses, the Communists now followed the strategy of neutralizing them. They sponsored the radical land-reform bill of 1945 and transformed overnight much of the agricultural proletatiat into a smallholding peasantry that, on the instant, turned against the Communist party in defense of its property rights. The remainder of the agricultural proletariat in the traditional areas of rural unrest was allowed to be organized into the fellow-traveling National Peasant party instead of the Communist party proper. The National Peasants were successfully manipulated from the outside then disbanded once the Communist seizure of power was complete. Within its own ranks the party dealt harshly with manifestations of agrarian radicalism. A group of young peasant zealots who advocated the immediate socialization of the economy and staged at least one anti-Semitic demonstration (by attempt to remove forcefully Jewish owners and managers of a large industrial plant) were shunted off the main tracks of party organization. They and other members of a potential or real agrarian opposition disappeared in the course of the post-1949 purges.

The agrarian opposition of the Soviet Republic was thus not a historically isolated, accidental phenomenon but the integral part of an ultraradical movement that had started at the time of the uprooting of village society in the nineteenth century and survived in various forms until the most recent years. This agrarian radicalism has displayed many similarities with the rural revolutionary movements of other east European countries and Russia. But even more strikingly, it offers many parallels with the character and operational concepts of many contemporary Communist movements in the lesser developed parts of the world, especially in Asia and Latin America.

Though agrarian communism in Hungary was inchoate and unorganized, one may still identify a number of traits it had in common with its latter-day counterparts: (1) a primitive chiliasm that was averse to dialectical thinking and doctrinal flexibility; (2) stress on voluntarism and the subjective factor of will over and above the analysis of objective social and economic factors; (3) a strong resistance to bureaucratic organization and routinized modes of action; and (4) a tendency to seek solidarities in terms of racial, national, and primary group identity.

Admittedly, the evidence at hand is too rudimentary to permit conclusions of great and global significance. But the example of the Hungarian agrarian "deviation" and its common traits with some contemporary Communist movements are interesting enough to suggest the urgency of cross-cultural inquiry into the impact of peasant cosmology and values on the character of revolution in the modern age. Under what circumstances these values will pervade the thinking of a Communist movement is hard to predict—Russia as well as Hungary in 1919 were agrarian countries after all, yet the urban trends prevailed in the revolutionary movements—but it appears that the question may become relevant in societies with a numerous and sufficiently mobilized agricultural proletariat. A contributing factor to the success of agrarian communism may be a belated process of economic development that brings about sharp differentiation between the agricultural and the urban proletariat and transforms the industrial workers into a privileged class, at least in the eyes of a dispossessed agricultural population. These conditions appear to have been present in countries like China and Cuba where the revolution followed a definitely agrarian trend by moving from a rural geographical and social base toward the cities thus reversing the earlier tendencies of European Communist revolutions.

In conclusion, the tentativeness of these propositions

and the necessity of further careful research will have to be once more emphasized. Should, however, the validity of these hypotheses be established with reasonable certainty, our understanding of conflict and pluralism in the Communist world would be enhanced. If indeed we found that the sources of current conflicts lie in different value systems rather than in the divergence of economic, military, and organizational interests, then the divisions among Communist states may be harder to reconcile and the divisions may persist for long periods to come, for then, in effect, we deal with two different political movements that by historical coincidence happen to carry the same label. For these reasons the exploration of agrarian radicalism in different cultural environments may become the most challenging task for the new wave of comparative research into the origin of Communist movements.

4

The Rumanian Socialists and the Hungarian Soviet Republic

Keith Hitchins

ONE OF the weaknesses of the Hungarian Soviet Republic and a cause of its early demise was its inability to deal effectively with the nationality problem which it had inherited from royal Hungary and the Károlyi government. It was unsuccessful in attracting any sizable numbers of non-Magyar Socialists, workers, and peasants to the cause of world proletarian revolution. Neither the Slovaks, nor the Serbs, nor the Rumanians of Hungary and Transylvania contributed to any important degree to the construction and defense of the Soviet Republic. The ephemeral Slovak Soviet Republic, proclaimed on June 16, 1919, was dominated by Magyars, while the Serbian and Rumanian Socialists who operated within the framework of the Hungarian Soviet Republic and the Hungarian Socialist or Communist parties represented only small fragments of their own Socialist parties, with which, in fact, they eventually severed all relations.

The inability of the Hungarian Soviet Republic to win the allegiance of the nationalities and thereby fulfill the historic role assigned to it by Béla Kun and the Russian Bolsheviks as a bridgehead of world revolution in Central Europe must not be laid to the negligence or ill will of Kun and his supporters. Although, in fact, they did devote little attention to the specifics of the nationality problem, more vigor on their part could hardly have overcome the strong separatist feelings of most Slovaks, Serbs, and Rumanians or of their Socialist parties. Concessions could not remove all the bitter memories of Magyarization which had accumulated in the preceding half-century. Moreover, the uneasy coalition of Communists and Social Democrats, formed on March 21, 1919 simultaneously with the proclamation of the Hungarian Soviet Republic, proved to be a serious handicap in dealing with the nationalities, because many prominent Social Democrats had made no secret of their eagerness to preserve the territorial integrity of Hungary and were, consequently, little inclined to appease the national feelings of others, whether they were Socialists or bourgeois. Although the majority of the non-Magyar Socialists of Hungary were undoubtedly influenced adversely by such continued manifestations of Magyar nationalism, their reasons for rejecting the Hungarian Soviet Republic must be sought mainly in their own strong national feeling. When the Habsburg monarchy disintegrated in the fall of 1918, they found it impossible to divorce themselves from the century-old movements of their peoples for national self-determination and, significantly enough, they judged their actions to be in complete harmony with the Socialist principles they had long espoused.

This chapter will concern itself with the efforts of Rumanian Socialists in Hungary and Transylvania to find solutions to the vital social and political questions posed by the disappearance of the Habsburg monarchy and the transformation of Hungary first into a bourgeois-democratic repub-

lic under Mihály Károlyi and then the proletarian dictatorship of Béla Kun and his followers, and will cover a period
from October 1918 to August 1919. The decisions which Rumanian Socialists eventually made were based upon the relative importance they assigned to national self-determination versus proletarian world revolution, and revolutionary
versus evolutionary social change. The pressure of events
proved to be greater than the fragile unity of their movement could bear, and it eventually broke up into three fairly
distinct groupings: the regular Social Democratic party,
which represented the overwhelming majority of Socialists
and workers; the Rumanian International Socialist faction,
which remained small in numbers and merged after a few
months' precarious existence with the third group, the Rumanian Communists, who advocated a total commitment to
world revolution and the establishment of the dictatorship
of the proletariat. On the basis of available published
sources it appears that national feeling largely determined
the policies of all three.

The revolutionary events of October and November
1918 obliged the leadership of the Rumanian Section of the
Social Democratic Party of Hungary, as the organization of
Rumanian Socialists in Hungary was then called, to take a
stand on basic issues of ideology and practical politics vital
to the future development of the Rumanian working-class
movement. In seeking social justice, they had to decide
whether to follow the example of Western European development and the teachings of Marxian socialism's greatest
theoretician in Rumania, Constantin Dobrogeanu-Gherea,
an evolutionist, or to adopt the tactics of revolutionary socialism, which had achieved such remarkable successes in
Soviet Russia; in attempting to solve the nationality problem, they might either remain within the new Hungarian

republic, which promised equal rights to all regardless of nationality, or choose union with the kingdom of Rumania and at the same time run the risk of political persecution and social oppression.

In defining their position on the future development of the Rumanians of Hungary and Transylvania and their own relationship to the Hungarian republic and the parent Hungarian Social Democratic party, Rumanian Socialist leaders found it impossible to separate the struggle for social justice and political liberty from the movement for self-determination. Their ideal, as it gradually took form between September and the end of November 1918, was the union of all Rumanians in a single state, in which their well-being would be assured and the will of the majority would be supreme. They regarded the poverty, the lack of education, and the political indifference of the overwhelming majority of Rumanian workers and peasants as the inevitable consequence of centuries of political fragmentation and foreign domination. Progress, they were convinced, would not be continually sapped by the struggle against national and social discrimination.

As it became increasingly clear that the old monarchy could not withstand much longer the pressure of its peoples —Germans and Magyars included—for relief from the hardships of war and for new forms of social and political organization which would guarantee their future prosperity, Rumanian Socialists attempted to strengthen their wing of the party by an intensive recruiting campaign among Rumanian workers and even peasants, whom, until recently, they had largely ignored. They were anxious to prepare themselves for the tasks which they believed history had assigned them: to overturn an unjust system and establish in its place a society in which every individual and every nation would be equal in rights and responsibilities.[1] Although Iosif Jumanca, the first secretary of the Rumanian section's executive committee, insisted that socialism was primarily a working-class movement which had as its basis the struggle between classes rather than nationalities, he impressed upon his colleagues the need to build a separate, Rumanian party. Only in this way, he argued, could large numbers of Rumanian workers in Hungary and Transylvania be drawn into the Socialist party and its trade unions. As things stood, many workers and intellectuals who accepted Socialist teachings about the evils of the present order of society shunned membership in the party out of fear that it would be the first step toward Magyarization. The predicament of the Rumanian worker who came from the village into the cosmopolitan atmosphere of the city, where a foreign culture and way of life predominated, was especially serious. Frequently his national identity was submerged in the Magyar-led trade union or local branch of the Socialist party. The only remedy, Jumanca admonished his colleagues, was increased activity on their part in establishing separate union groups and party sections and in providing better opportunities for the workers to study their own language and history.[2]

The Rumanian Socialists' response to the plight of the Rumanian peasant also combined class struggle with national feeling. The responsibility for the backwardness of the peasants, they argued in an indirect criticism of the Rumanian National party, rested partly upon those who had up to then acted as their leaders and who had failed to give them a proper political education. The principal cause, however, they discovered in the desire of the "masters of the country"

---

[1] *Adevărul* (The Truth), August 12–25, 1918.
[2] *Ibid.*

to keep the peasants ignorant and poor so that they could the more easily manage them. Although they named Rumanians as well as Magyars in their indictment, it was clear that "masters" referred to Magyar landlords, who were more numerous and wealthier than their Rumanian counterparts, and to the traditional Hungarian political parties. Although they admitted that a few Rumanian businessmen and landlords, moved by feelings of compassion for their people, had helped here and there, their efforts had been limited by their own class interests, which would never allow them to endanger their own economic and political power.[3] Rumanian Socialists concluded, therefore, that only their party was genuinely interested in raising the living standards of the working masses. For a brief time, however, they remained uncertain about which tactic would be more effective—an appeal to class consciousness or to national solidarity.

As the monarchy approached its end, the general outlines of a program gradually emerged. By the beginning of October, Rumanian Socialists had come to the conclusion that the old order of society was beyond salvation and that the traditional ruling classes—the landed aristocracy and most elements of the bourgeoisie—thoroughly discredited by their war policies, were incapable by their nature of building and providing the leadership for a new world. These tasks, therefore, would devolve upon the Socialists and other "democratic elements." Their main concern during the next two months was to select the most suitable environment in which a strong Rumanian working-class movement might develop and in which they themselves could contribute most effectively to the creation of a free and democratic society. They had three choices: a democratic

[3] *Ibid.*, August 19–September 1, 1918.

Hungary; an independent state comprising Transylvania and the areas of Hungary and the Banat inhabited by Rumanians; or the kingdom of Rumania. They eventually settled on the one which they believed offered the majority of the Rumanian people the fullest freedom in determining their own future.

At first, Rumanian Socialists seemed to waver on the question of separation from Hungary. On the one hand, they approved the Hungarian Social Democratic party's manifesto of October to the non-Magyar peoples of Hungary which promised them full citizenship and social justice in the hope that they would accept Hungary as their homeland and would not try to dismember it; on the other hand, they heartily endorsed a proposal made at the special congress of the Hungarian Social Democratic party on October 13 by Zsigmond Kunfi, a leading Socialist who was to become minister of welfare in the Károlyi government, that the Magyars permit their brother Socialists to secede from Hungary if they failed to establish a country in which the rights of all regardless of nationality were respected; if Magyars were to be condemned to injustice and oppression, Kunfi argued, then at least the nationalities ought to be granted their freedom. The ambiguities in the Rumanian Socialists' attitude persisted until mid-October, as they continued to express the hope that Hungary might somehow become a "Switzerland of the East" and to warn at the same time that if the ruling classes prevented this, then the Hungary they had known would be completely swept away.[4] This suggests that they had serious doubts about the future of the nationalities in Hungary. In this address to the congress, Ioan Flueraş, with Jumanca the chief spokesman of the Rumanians, opposed any cooperation between the Socialists and the

---

[4] *Ibid.*, October 6–20, 1918.

Hungarian bourgeois parties.[5] He and his colleagues were worried that Magyar Socialists, as the price of a coalition government, might be persuaded to accept the nationality policies of the bourgeois parties, which were desperately seeking ways to preserve Hungary's territorial integrity. The Rumanians evidently hoped that somehow the Socialists by themselves could establish a democratic regime which would carry out both the far-reaching social and political reforms and the promises of self-determination to the non-Magyar peoples provided for in the party program.

As the political situation in the monarchy continued to deteriorate, Rumanian Socialist leaders began to conceive of self-determination in terms of a union or federation of all Rumanians of Hungary, Transylvania, the Banat, Bukovina, Bessarabia, and the old kingdom. In their view Rumanian workers and Socialists, wherever they lived, formed a part of the Rumanian nation, and as such their future depended upon the actions and the will of the whole. Consequently, they realized that their party might be obliged to work with individuals and groups of widely divergent social and political views, but denied that they themselves need abandon their own principles in the process. According to this line of reasoning, cooperation with Rumanian bourgeois parties was not only permitted—it was considered essential.

The decisive moment in the development of their policy came when they offered to meet with representatives of the Rumanian National party in Budapest to discuss the future of their nation. At their conference on October 29 Flueraş, and Ioan Mihuţ, a member of the Socialist execu-

---

[5] *A magyar munkásmozgalom történetének válogatott dokumentumai* (Selected Documents on the History of the Hungarian Working-class Movement), (November 7, 1917–March 21, 1919), (Budapest: Szikra, 1956), V, 252.

tive committee, urged the Rumanian National party to join
the Socialists in establishing a Rumanian National Council,
which would assume administrative responsibility for the
areas of Hungary inhabited by Rumanians and represent
them in negotiations with the Hungarian government and
the Magyar National Council.[6] On the morning of October
31, in the midst of the revolution that was to bring the
Magyar National Council to power and install Károlyi as
minister-president of a new, democratic government, the
Rumanian National Council, consisting of six Socialists and
six representatives of the Rumanian National party, was
formed. Although the Socialists recognized the National
Council as the representative of the Rumanians of Hungary
and Transylvania, they regarded it as provisional, to be replaced by permanent institutions as soon as the people themselves had had an opportunity to express their wishes.[7]
Within a week the council had left Budapest and had established itself in Arad, where it would be nearer the com-
pact masses of Rumanians in Transylvania and could more
easily coordinate the activities of the numerous local national councils that were being formed throughout Transylvania. It also undertook to replace Magyar officials with
Rumanians in those places where Rumanians constituted a
majority of the population and to establish a Rumanian
national guard to maintain order.[8]

During the rest of November relations between the
Rumanian Socialists, on the one hand, and the Károlyi government and the leadership of the Hungarian Social Democratic party, on the other, became increasingly strained.
Flueraş and his colleagues had great respect for Károlyi and

---

[6] Tiron Albani, *Douăzeci de ani dela unire* (Twenty Years since the
Union), (Oradea: Grafica, 1938), I, 167–168.

[7] *Adevărul*, October 28–November 10, 1918.

[8] Albani, *op. cit.*, pp. 170–171.

regarded him as a sincere and honest politician, but they also doubted that he could exert much influence upon the policies of his own government, because he lacked a strong political party of his own or a mass following. Although they believed that he personally desired a just solution of the nationality problem, they had no illusions about the determination of the Magyar bourgeois parties to defend Hungary's historical boundaries at all costs.[9] Moreover, the composition of the Magyar National Council in Budapest and the various local national councils in Transylvania, particularly the one in Cluj, which had among their members well-known nationalists and conservatives, caused Rumanian Socialists grave misgivings about the future of their people and the prospects of achieving socialism in the new Hungary. It seemed to them that Hungarian Socialists, in accepting what amounted to a junior partnership in the new government and by abandoning, if only temporarily, the independent pursuit of working-class goals, had forfeited the fruits of a half-century of struggle.

The failure later on of the negotiations between a Hungarian government delegation headed by Oscar Jászi, minister without portfolio in charge of national questions, and representatives of the Rumanian National Council merely increased the Rumanian Socialists' disenchantment with the policies of the Hungarian republic and the parent Social Democratic party. They were appalled by the inclusion in the Hungarian delegation of István Apáthy, representing the Magyar National Council of Transylvania, whom they regarded as a leading member of the oligarchy that had just been overthrown and a chauvinist, and refused to take part in the conference until Jászi had assured them that Apáthy would be present as an observer only.[10] The

---

[9] *Adevărul,* October 6–20, 1918.

[10] Albani, *op. cit.,* p. 191.

actual negotiations, which took place in Arad between November 12 and 15, collapsed over questions of boundaries and territory. Jászi's compromise plan for the establishment of autonomous Magyar and Rumanian enclaves in those areas where it was impossible to determine ethnic boundaries was rejected by both the representatives of the Rumanian National party and the Socialists. The discussions ended on a bitter note, when Dezsö Bokány, a member of the executive committee of the Hungarian Social Democratic party, threatened to take action against the Rumanian Socialists within the Socialist International unless they accepted the enclave plan. This and the general attitude of Hungarian Socialists at the conference convinced the Rumanian Socialists that they were as nationalistic as the middle classes and that it would be useless to treat with them further on such questions.[11]

Rumanian Socialist leaders had undoubtedly by this time decided that union with Rumania was their only reasonable course of action, but it is clear that they faced this decision with misgivings. The social and political system in Rumania repelled them. Although they professed a strong desire to see the Rumanian people united, they could not ignore the miserable state of the working class in Rumania and its utter neglect by middle-class politicians and landlords, who, they claimed, used political and economic power for their own selfish ends.[12] They had also to consider a question of international Socialist principle, of which their Magyar colleagues in Budapest continually reminded them: could they in good conscience desert a democratic republic, in which the broadest liberty prevailed, for a kingdom with a long record of class oppression, even though it was of their nationality? Such considerations led them to insist that

---

[11] *Ibid.*, 193, 196.
[12] *Adevărul*, November 5–17, 1918; November 12–24, 1918.

Transylvania and the other areas of Hungary inhabited by Rumanians remain autonomous until there were sufficient guarantees that Rumania would become a democratic country and that its leaders would enact constitutional and agrarian reforms guaranteeing the people their well-being and a dominant voice in managing their own affairs.[13] Their determination to support eventual union with Rumania, if this was the will of the Rumanian people, did not, however, waver.

In order to have as broad an expression of public opinion as possible, they took the initiative in organizing the national assembly of Alba Iulia. Here, on December 1, 1918, more than one hundred thousand Rumanians from every part of Transylvania, the Banat, and adjoining areas of Hungary overwhelmingly approved union with the kingdom of Rumania. The sixty official delegates of the Rumanian Socialists, including Flueraş and Jumanca, also voted for union, but only after the Rumanian National Council had accepted some conditions. That they supported union, in spite of their strong reservations, was due primarily to their belief that it was the duty of social democracy to assist every people to develop in accordance with its own traditions and desires. In particular, they felt a deep moral responsibility to work for the liberation and union of their own people, because they believed that it could progress materially and spiritually only within the framework of a national state. Their vote for union was also an expression of their concern about the future of the Rumanian Socialist movement. They were convinced that their failure to support what the majority of Rumanians so ardently desired would have brought them into disrepute and would have

---

[13] *Ibid.,* November 5–17, November 12–24, November 19–December 1, 1918; Albani, *op. cit.,* pp. 165, 172–173.

deprived them of any significant influence among the Rumanian working classes for generations to come. They were equally convinced that an active, well-organized Socialist party in Greater Rumania would serve as the best guarantee of the country's transformation into a democratic republic and, consequently, were unwilling to forsake this role by remaining in Budapest as a mere adjunct of the Hungarian Social Democratic party.[14] They made their intentions public on December 2 by accepting membership in the Consiliu Dirigent, a sort of provisional government which was to administer Transylvania until its final status and boundaries had been settled, and by changing the name of the party to Social Democratic party of Transylvania and by moving its headquarters from Budapest to Sibiu.

In the four months between the proclamation of union with Rumania on December 1, 1918 and the establishment of the Hungarian Soviet Republic on March 21, 1919, Rumanian Socialists plunged enthusiastically into the work of constructing a new democratic Rumania. They were proud of the fact that their party, and through it the working class, would at last have a decisive voice in the affairs of their country and would cease to be merely a faction within the Hungarian Social Democratic party.[15] They were confident that broad social and political changes could take place rapidly within the framework of the national state and that the proper agent for this was a united Rumanian Socialist party. To this end they urged fellow Socialists in the old kingdom, Bukovina, and Bessarabia to join them in seeking ways to consolidate their separate parties into a single powerful organization capable of leading the reform movement and of resisting the forces of reaction which had al-

---

[14] *Adevărul*, December 2–15, 1918, January 13–26, 1919.
[15] *Ibid.*, January 6–19, 1919.

ready begun to assert themselves.[16] More determined than ever to support the ideal of Greater Rumania as the only setting within which the Rumanian people might hope to achieve complete self-fulfillment, they now gave public utterance for the first time to the indignation they felt over the status of the Rumanians in old Hungary. Emil Isac, a poet and newspaper editor of Transylvania, expressed their feelings best in the spirited reply he published in *Adevărul* (The Truth), the party organ, to a Hungarian Socialist who had questioned the sincerity of their commitment to socialism and democracy because of their support of the union of Transylvania with Rumania. The union, Isac declared, was necessary for the development of the Rumanian people and signified their emancipation from foreign rule. If this had happened several hundred years earlier, they would now be a numerous and cultivated people able to serve all humanity rather than an inert mass, subjugated and politically unconscious. In supporting the union, Rumanian Socialists had not sacrificed their principles for a cheap chauvinist success. On the contrary, they wanted the new Rumania to be a free, democratic country where the Rumanian people could enter fully into the civilized life of Europe rather than remain a negligible quantity divided among several states and dissipating their energies in resisting oppression.[17]

In spite of their eagerness for change, Rumanian Socialists reluctantly admitted that Rumania was not yet ready for a Socialist revolution. In their view, capitalism had barely struck root, and the bourgeois-democratic state, which would provide the necessary conditions for its full development, had still to be built.[18] They tended to ignore the rev-

---

[16] *Ibid.*, February 24–March 9, 1919.
[17] *Ibid.*, February 3–16, 1919.
[18] Albani, *op. cit.*, pp. 110–111.

olutionary lessons being taught by the Bolsheviks in Russia and sought their models in Western Europe. They believed in an orderly evolution of society through parliamentary democracy and cooperation with progressive bourgeois political parties on the basis of universal suffrage and freedom of expression and assembly. They did not, however, abandon their own program of reform and pressed for the socialization of all major industrial enterprises, better conditions for the worker, agrarian reform, and a thorough revision of the tax system.[19]

As time passed, Rumanian Socialists immersed themselves in the problems of the new Rumania and strove to integrate their own party and trade-union organizations into those of the old kingdom. Their remaining tenuous links with the Hungarian government and Hungarian Socialists, already strained by mutual recriminations, were finally severed at the beginning of March 1919 when the Consiliu Dirigent recalled its representatives from Budapest in retaliation for the Hungarian government's alleged persecution of Rumanian officials and acquiescence in the pillaging of Rumanian villages.[20] Thus, by the time the Hungarian Soviet Republic came into being the largest body of Rumanian Socialists and the overwhelming majority of Rumanian workers whom they represented had already officially divorced themselves from Hungary and Hungarian social democracy.

Not all Rumanian Socialists approved the incorporation of Transylvania into Rumania and cooperation with the Rumanian National party. In the weeks preceding the national assembly at Alba Iulia, a number of groups and in-

---

[19] *Adevărul*, January 6–19, January 20–February 2, 1919.
[20] *Ibid.*, February 24–March 9, 1919.

dividuals, particularly in the Banat, actively campaigned against union with Rumania until it had in fact become a democratic republic.[21] The dissidents, however, were too few in number and too loosely organized to influence the final decision. Recognizing their weakness and encouraged by certain Hungarian Socialists,[22] they convened a so-called Congress of Rumanian Internationalists in Budapest on December 31, 1918 and January 1, 1919 to establish a formal organization. Although they succeeded in giving themselves a name—the Rumanian International Socialist Faction of Transylvania, the Banat, and Hungary—and in publishing a weekly newspaper, *Glasul Poporului* (The Voice of the People)—their activities were largely restricted to Budapest and Hungary proper, and they exercised little influence over the Rumanian working class generally.

Their program, as expressed in editorials in the party organ, differed in several important respects from that of the regular Rumanian Socialist organization. They were irrevocably opposed to the union of Transylvania with Rumania—and to the Serbian occupation of the Banat as well—on the grounds that this meant the extension of the power of the bourgeoisie and the landlords over peoples who had only recently liberated themselves from the Hungarian oligarchy. They accused the capitalists and landlords of Rumania in particular of seeking only to enslave the people of Transylvania and pointed to the peasant uprising of 1907, in which nearly 11,000 peasants had been killed, as an example of what they could expect from their union with Rumania.[23] They castigated Flueraş, Jumanca, and their supporters for agreeing to cooperate with the Rumanian

---

[21] Albani, *op. cit.*, pp. 206–207.

[22] *Adevărul*, December 30, 1918–January 12, 1919.

[23] *Glasul Poporului* (The Voice of the People), February 2, 1919.

National party, whose leaders' chief interest in creating a Greater Rumania was, in their view, to preserve their own wealth and privileges. Bourgeois nationalists were, consequently, the worst enemies of the proletariat, and the perpetuation of their rule would bring neither peace nor prosperity to the working classes.[24] For similar reasons the Internationalists doubted the ability of the Károlyi government to satisfy the aspirations of the peoples of Transylvania and the Banat.

The Internationalists were also deeply concerned about the nationality problem, but considered both the Rumanian and Hungarian middle classes incapable of solving it. They therefore advocated the transformation of Transylvania and the Banat into an independent federal republic, based upon the Swiss cantonal system, in which all nationalities would share political power and responsibilities equally.[25] Under this plan the people themselves—Serbs, Magyars, and Szeklers as well as Rumanians—would establish their own institutions unhindered by the presence of Rumanian and Serbian troops.

The Internationalists assumed that the possibility of a Socialist revolution in the new republic (they were certain that this would be the choice of the people) was remote and that a long period of struggle with the bourgeoisie was inevitable. Like the Social Democrats in Sibiu, they were essentially evolutionary in their thought and concentrated their immediate attention upon organization and propaganda within the existing political and social framework. Regarding themselves as the only true leaders of the pro-

---

[24] *Ibid.*, February 16, 1919.

[25] *Ibid.*, February 2, 1919; George Avramescu, the editor of *Glasul Poporului*, expressed the same sentiments as a delegate to the congress of the Hungarian Social Democratic party in Budapest on February 9, 1919. See *Glasul Poporului*, February 16, 1919.

letariat, they were determined to strengthen its class consciousness and to provide it with unions and a political party
capable of wresting power from the bourgeoisie. Their ultimate objective was the definitive emancipation of the
working class, but not by promises of universal suffrage and
the distribution of land to the peasants, which they regarded
as crumbs offered by bourgeois liberals to mislead the workers. They expected a transformation of existing society, in
which a relatively few individuals possessed most of the
wealth, into one in which those who worked owned the
means of production and used them for the benefit of all.[26]
Although this sounded revolutionary, the Internationalists
failed to offer any detailed plan how these objectives might
be achieved. In spite of the bellicose tone of their writings,
they made no appeal to violence and insisted that peaceful
evolution, "as Marx advocated," was the proper means to
their ends.[27]

The International Socialist Faction seems to have led a
precarious existence from its inception. Its vagueness on
tactics, its neglect of peasant aspirations, and its failure to
appreciate the power of nationalism deprived it of any mass
following among Rumanians,[28] and an equivocal nationality policy discouraged cooperation with Hungarian Socialists and Communists. Its leaders, with a few exceptions, were
minor figures in the Rumanian Socialist movement. Many
of them, in fact, had come from Rumania after the peasant
uprising of 1907 and were less affected by the nationality
struggle in Hungary than were the native Transylvanians.[29]
Competition from the left wing eventually proved too

[26] *Ibid.*, March 2, 1919.

[27] *Ibid.*, February 9, 1919.

[28] The Social Democrats made a severe indictment of the faction in
Adevărul, December 23, 1918–January 5, 1919.

[29] Albani, *op. cit.*, p. 206.

strong to resist, and a few days after the proclamation of the Hungarian Soviet Republic the Internationalists merged with the Rumanian Communist group. Their participation in the new organization was far from passive, however, and was the cause of much strife over policy and tactics.

Rumanian Communists, who had been active in Hungary and Transylvania as an organized body since November 1918, were the most radical element in the Rumanian Socialist movement and, consequently, the most enthusiastic supporters of the Hungarian Soviet republic. Many had been Social Democrats, and during the war, while serving in the Austro-Hungarian army on the eastern front, had been captured and interned in Russia. In the summer of 1918 they began to return home from prisoner-of-war camps in Russia, where, through work in factories and on farms side-by-side with Russian workers and peasants, through service in the Red Army, and through involvement in a succession of organizations sponsored by the Russian Bolsheviks, they had served their revolutionary apprenticeship. Inspired by the success of their Russian tutors, they became fervent believers in the imminence of world revolution.[30] A particularly important influence upon their later activities was their close collaboration with Hungarian Social Democrats in various cities in eastern and southern Russia in the spring and summer of 1918. The most important of their joint organizations was the Magyar-Rumanian group of the Inter-

---

[30] Their experiences in Russia are described in Keith Hitchins, "The Russian Revolution and the Rumanian Socialist Movement, 1917–1918," *Slavic Review*, XXVII:2 (June 1968), 278–281, and Gheorghe Unc, *Solidarnost' rumynskogo rabochego i demokraticheskogo dvizheniia s Velikom Oktiabr'skoi Sotsialisticheskoi Revoliutsiei (1917–1922)*, (The Solidarity of Rumanian Workers and the Democratic Movement with the Great October Socialist Revolution [1917–1922]), (Bucharest: Editura Academiei R.S.R., 1968), 65–89.

national Social Democratic Workers party in Omsk, which by May 1918 had reached a membership of 3,200. Aided by local Bolshevik organizations, it carried on an intensive propaganda campaign among former prisoners of war in order to prepare them for the tasks of revolution when they returned home. This collaboration between Hungarian and Rumanian Social Democrats was natural, inasmuch as the Rumanian section of the party in Hungary had operated under the general supervision of the parent organization. Rumanian Socialists and radicals from Hungary and Transylvania had their own organizations in Russia, too. One of the most active was the Rumanian Revolutionary Peasant party, founded in Moscow in January 1918 by former prisoners of war, most of whom were peasants from Transylvania. Its main activity was propaganda work, carried on directly in the camps by its members, who received specialized training at a political school established in Moscow by the Bolshevik Central Committee, and in the columns of the party newspaper, *Foaia Țăranului* (The Peasant's Journal).

Large numbers of former prisoners of war began to return home after the signing of the peace treaty of Brest-Litovsk between Russia and the Central Powers on March 3, 1918, but only a few actually retained their revolutionary enthusiasm. The Hungarian Communist party, founded on November 24, 1918, attempted to establish nationality sections composed of those who had participated in party organizations in Russia, and the party organ, *Vörös Újság,* in its issue of December 21, 1918, urgently requested Communist groups of all nationalities returning from Russia

---

[31] V. Cheresteşiu, "Pătrunderea ideilor Marii Revoluţii Socialiste din Octombrie în masele din Transilvania" (The Penetration of the Ideas of the Great October Socialist Revolution among the Masses of Transylvania), *Anuarul Institutului de Istorie din Cluj,* I–II (1958–1959), 253–254.

to report to the party secretariat in Budapest as soon as possible.[32]

With the support of Hungarian Communists, Rumanian repatriates from Russia, joined by a few dissident Socialists in Budapest, formed a Rumanian Communist faction in November 1918.[33] A more formal organization came into being a month later, also under the aegis of the Hungarian Communist party. On December 26, at party headquarters in Budapest, a small group of militants constituted themselves the Rumanian Communist Group of Budapest and approved a ten-point program reminiscent in language and intent of similar Russian and Hungarian Communist manifestoes. Briefly, it demanded the immediate confiscation of all lands and farm inventory belonging to the church and large and middle-sized landlords and of all banks, factories, mines, and other industries, which henceforth were to be operated by peasants and workers; the disarming of the regular army, the gendarmerie, and the police, and their replacement by armed workers and peasants; the introduction of obligatory labor for all on the theory that only he who worked should eat; the immediate separation of church and state; and, finally, the transfer of state power to councils (*sfaturi*) of workers, peasants, and soldiers and the immediate establishment of a dictatorship of the proletariat.[34]

The spirit which pervaded this manifesto as well as the editorials in the new party organ, *Steagul Roşu* (The Red Banner), with their terseness of language and matter-of-fact

[32] Rudolf L. Tökés, *Béla Kun and the Hungarian Soviet Republic* (New York: Praeger, 1967), 106, n. 20.

[33] *Revoluţia Socială* (The Social Revolution), June 26, 1919.

[34] *Documente din istoria Partidului Comunist din România, 1917–1922* (Documents concerning the History of the Communist Party of Rumania), I (2nd ed.; Bucharest: Editura pentru literatura politică, 1956), 110–111.

prescriptions for the reordering of society, had not been present before in the Rumanian Socialist movement in Hungary—not even among the Internationalists—and must be attributed mainly to the experiences of the group's members in Russia and their close association with Hungarian Communists at home. They had adopted the views held by Béla Kun that the proletarian revolution would not be confined to Russia alone, but would soon spread to Germany and eventually to all Europe. They believed that conditions for revolution in Hungary were ripe and that it was, moreover, inevitable because it was the only means they could conceive of by which the contradictions inherent in capitalist society could be eliminated. The prospects for the quick victory of socialism made them contemptuous of the reformist tactics advocated by the Rumanian Social Democratic party. In brutal language they denounced Flueraş and Jumanca as traitors to the proletariat because of their "alliance" with the bourgeoisie of Transylvania. They claimed that their actions were typical of Social Democratic tactics everywhere, which aimed at the preservation of "putrid" capitalist society by means of bourgeois-democratic republics and had brought the international working-class movement "to the edge of the abyss," and recommended as a method of dealing with them the Russian Bolsheviks' treatment of the Mensheviks and other gradualists. They considered the creation of a true revolutionary party patterned after that of the Bolsheviks to be their first task in throwing off the "capitalist yoke" and instituting a dictatorship of the proletariat.[35]

The Rumanian Communist Group vigorously pressed these points at the congress of Rumanian Socialists organized by the Internationalists in Budapest on December 31,

---

[35] *Ibid.*, 107–109.

1918 and January 1, 1919. Its members, in fact, dominated the meeting and won approval of their program over that proposed by the more moderate Internationalists. A united party, however, did not immediately come into being because of fundamental differences regarding the merits of revolution relative to evolution and the degree of national autonomy individual Socialist parties might enjoy within the international working-class movement. It is remarkable that the spokesman for the Rumanian Communist Group—and, apparently, its leaders as well[36]—was a Henrik Kagan, identified as a Russian and the former commander of a Rumanian revolutionary battalion in Russia. It was he who on the first day led the attack on the Social Democrats and, on the second, explained the Communist program and moved its adoption as binding on all true socialists.[37] The Hungarian Communist party also took an active part in the congress. Ernö Pór, a member of the party's central committee in charge of propaganda activities in Slovakia, appealed to the revolutionary fervor of the delegates by predicting the imminent collapse of capitalism and the outbreak of world revolution, by extolling the achievements of the Russian proletariat and denouncing the treachery of the Social Democrats, and by urging his listeners to join forces with their brother Russian, German, Hungarian, and Austrian Communist parties.[38]

Rumanian Communists together with a few members of the International Socialist Faction had their first opportunity to experiment on a large scale with social revolution in Bihar County and its chief city, Oradea, between January and April 1919. In the process the effectiveness of interna-

---

[36] *A magyar munkásmozgalom*, V, 433. "The Report of an Investigation of Tibor Szamuely's Activities," January 15, 1919.

[37] *Ibid.*, 424; account contained in *Vörös Újság*, January 4, 1919.

[38] *Ibid.*

tional proletarian solidarity was severely tested. Their principal activity was agitation among those peasants who had insufficient plots of land or none at all, and worked as day laborers on large and middle-sized estates. They also made a determined effort to reestablish contact with the thousands of soldiers returning home from Russia and to rekindle their revolutionary enthusiasm. Several organizations composed of these elements operated under the supervision of the Rumanian Communist Group of Oradea. The most important was the Rumanian Revolutionary Peasant party, which had its own newspaper, *Foaia Țăranului*. Both names indicate that the party's membership was drawn mainly from repatriates from Russia. Another organization, which devoted its attention to the poorest segment of the peasantry, called itself the Committee of Ploughmen and Workers.[39]

The leaflets and brochures which these groups distributed in the villages were unabashedly Bolshevik in tone and content. A good example is a booklet titled *Potrăcarii*, originally published in Moscow by the Rumanian Group of the Russian Communist party in December 1918 and reprinted by the Rumanian Revolutionary Peasant party in Oradea in January or February 1919. It declared the first task of all Rumanian revolutionaries to be the formation of an alliance between the proletariat and the poorer peasantry as a prelude to the seizure of power. After this had been accomplished soviets of workers' and peasants' deputies would supervise the socialization of all land and the means of production and ensure their use for the benefit of those who worked.[40] The editorials in *Foaia Țăranului*, which bore the

---

[39] One of their leaflets is reproduced in Roman R. Ciorogariu, *Zile trăite* (Days Endured), (Oradea: Tipografia diecezana, 1926), 193.

[40] Fl. Dragne, "Momente din activitatea desfășurată la sate de mili-

same slogans on its masthead as its predecessor in Moscow—
"Țărani și muncitori din lumea întreagă, uniți-vă!" (Peasants and Workers of the World, Unite) and "Pace colibelor,
război curților domnești!" (Peace to the Cottages, War to
the Manor Houses)—dwelt at length upon the "decadence
and corruption" of Rumanian society and the inevitability
of revolutionary upheaval, upon the wickedness of Mensheviks, Socialist Revolutionaries, and Populists, who as "servants of the bourgeoisie" prolonged the life of the capitalist
system, and upon the valuable lessons to be learned from
the experiences of the Russian proletariat.[41] Some editorials
warned Magyar and Rumanian peasants and workers to be-
ware of so-called patriots who preached national defense
and self-determination, for these people were in reality
landlords and capitalists who used this device to divide and
weaken the forces of revolution. Rumanian workers had, in
fact, every reason to join hands with their magyar comrades, for the cause of their suffering was the common class
enemy, whether Rumanian or Magyar.[42]

The Rumanian Communist Group and its affiliated organizations in Oradea received only limited support from
their Magyar colleagues. Although Béla Kun himself visited
Oradea in February 1919, bringing with him two Rumanian Communists from Budapest, Gustav Auerbach and N.
Kornstein, to organize the Rumanian revolutionary movement in Transylvania,[43] there does not seem to have been

---

tanții aripii revoluționare a mișcării muncitorești în frunte cu grupur-
ile comuniste (1917–1921)" (Aspects of the Activity Undertaken in the
Villages by Militants Belonging to the Revolutionary Wing of the
Working-class Movement led by Communist Groups), *Studii și ma-
teriale de istorie contemporană,* II (Bucharest: Editura Academiei
R.P.R., 1962), 20–21.

[41] *Foaia Țăranului* (The Peasant's Journal), March 22, 1919.

[42] *Ibid.,* March 7, 1919.

[43] Ciorogariu, *op. cit.,* p. 217.

close collaboration between the Rumanians and the dominant Magyar organizations or even a satisfactory liaison between the Oradea group and Rumanian Communist headquarters in Budapest. A Rumanian, Iacob Crețulescu, did indeed serve on the Workers Council for Bihar County in April 1919, but none of his colleagues seem to have been entrusted with such important responsibilities.[44] The general impression one gains of the Rumanian Communists' efforts in Bihar is one of impotence and disorganization. They not only failed to attract a mass following, but actually alienated the majority of the peasantry by insisting upon the rapid collectivization of land, by attacking the church, to which most peasants were deeply attached, and by disregarding the power of nationalism.

The proclamation of the Hungarian Soviet Republic on March 21, 1919, aroused the revolutionary enthusiasm of both Rumanian Communists and Internationalists. Inspired by the union of the Hungarian Communist and Social Democratic parties, they, too, formed a single organization on March 23, which they initially named the Rumanian Socialist party of Hungary.[45] The new party hailed the establishment of the Hungarian Soviet Republic as the dawn of a new era of liberty for all the working people of Hungary and as the death blow to the bourgeoisie,[46] and predicted that the proletarian revolution would quickly spread to all of Europe with Hungary serving as a bridge between Russia

---

[44] Dezsö Farkas, *A két forradalom Bihar megyei történetéhez 1917–1919* (Contributions to the History of the Two Revolutions of Bihar County), (Budapest: Akadémiai Kiadó, 1965), p. 83. Farkas, who did some of the research for his book in Rumania, is silent about the activities of the Rumanian revolutionaries.

[45] *Glasul Poporului,* March 27, 1919.

[46] *Ibid.,* March 23, 1919.

and the West. It demanded the total transformation of society and warned that it would not tolerate a regime half-capitalist and half-socialist.[47] This all-or-nothing attitude on the major issues of the day was evident in all the party's publications, including its newspaper, *Revoluția Socială* (The Social Revolution),[48] but was not solely destructive. In the early weeks of the Republic, particularly, Rumanian Communists[49] praised its work of reconstruction and innovation as essential for the success of the revolution,[50] and their party organ dutifully published the decrees of the new regime and the speeches of its leaders.

Rumanian Communists continually contrasted the happy state of affairs in Hungary with the "foul politics, abject morals, and enslavement of the people," which, they claimed, characterized life in Rumania.[51] They insisted that the working class in Rumania had never known true freedom and had enjoyed only such rights as those of paying exorbitant taxes, dying of hunger, going to jail, or shedding blood in capitalist wars, and offered as the only alternative the dictatorship of the proletariat.[52] They enthusiastically predicted that the day of revolution was near at hand. The initial purpose of all this was to dissuade Rumanian workers

[47] *Revoluția Socială*, April 15, 1919.

[48] *Revoluția Socială* was the successor to *Glasul Poporului* and was published from March 29 to August 3, 1919. Through the issue of April 15 it called itself "Organ of the Rumanian Socialist Party of Hungary"; from then through the issue of June 15 the word "Socialist" was replaced by "Communist"; the final fourteen issues appeared as the "Rumanian Organ of the Socialist-Communist Party of Hungary."

[49] This term will also include those individuals, like the Internationalists, who collaborated with the Communists but who did not actually join their party.

[50] *Revoluția Socială*, March 29, 1919.

[52] *Ibid.*, April 1, 1919.

and peasants in Transylvania from supporting the union
with Rumania; and when, in the last two weeks of April, the
Rumanian army began to advance into Bihar County and
Hungary proper as far as the Tisza River, Rumanian Communists organized meetings of protest and condemned the
action as a "criminal attack by the armies of Rumanian imperialism" against Hungarian territory.[53] They appealed to
Rumanian soldiers to turn their weapons against their real
enemies who were using them to transplant the "tyrannical
rule of the Balkans" to Transylvania.[54]

However great the admiration of Rumanian Communists for the Hungarian Soviet Republic as the harbinger of
revolution in Central Europe may have been, their true
model and inspiration was Soviet Russia. They placed their
own revolutionary movement in a broader context than
simply that of the fate of Transylvania. They were no more
willing than their Social Democratic enemies in Sibiu to
remain a mere appendage of a Hungarian Socialist or Communist party. They applauded the federalist solution of the
nationality problem provided for in the constitution of the
Russian republic and, as time passed, gave far more attention to the theoretical writings of Russian Bolsheviks like
Nikolai Bukharin and Karl Radek and the directives of the
Communist International than to the pronouncements of
Béla Kun and his associates.[55] The maximum goal of their
own movement was to extend revolution to all the lands inhabited by Rumanians and to bring about their eventual
amalgamation into a Rumanian Soviet Republic, and they
regarded Soviet Russia and its Red Army as the chief guar-

---

[53] *Ibid.*, May 1, 8, and 29, 1919.
[54] *Ibid.*, May 22, 1919.
[55] See, for example, *Revoluţia Socială*, March 29, April 3, April 5, 1919.

antors of their success.[56] In the struggle for Bessarabia between the Rumanian and Red armies they never wavered in their support of the latter and of those Rumanian revolutionaries like Christian Rakovsky, who, they predicted, would march victoriously across the Prut River at the head of a Rumanian workers' army and establish a dictatorship of the proletariat.[57]

The Rumanian Communists' attachment to Russia grew even stronger in the spring of 1919, as serious differences developed between them and the Hungarian Socialist-Communist coalition. The Rumanians deeply resented their lack of independence and what they considered to be the outright neglect of their special national interests by their Hungarian colleagues. Both sides must share responsibility for the quarrel. Kun certainly recognized the importance of a just solution of the nationality problem and was eager to win the support of the non-Magyar peoples for the Hungarian revolution. He also assumed that the Hungarian Soviet Republic would serve as a catalyst for proletarian revolution throughout Eastern Europe and expended considerable effort on propaganda work in Slovakia, the Serbian areas of southern Hungary, and Transylvania. In his famous letter of March 11, 1919, to Ignác Bogár, head of the Printers' Union, Kun categorically rejected the policy of defending Hungary's territorial integrity as simply a means devised by the bourgeoisie to promote collaboration between classes and thereby undermine working-class solidarity.[58] He was willing to grant the non-Magyar nationalities a broad measure of autonomy, but refused to recognize their

[56] *Ibid.*, April 27, 1919.

[57] *Ibid.*, April 1, July 13, 1919.

[58] Béla Kun, A magyar Tanácsköztársaságról (On the Hungarian Soviet Republic), (Budapest: Kossuth, 1958), pp. 139–148.

right to secede from Hungary. He believed that the establishment of a dictatorship of the proletariat would of itself bring a solution to the nationality problem and that in any case the non-Magyars would find their existence in a Hungarian Soviet Republic preferable to life under Rumanian, Serbian, or Czech bourgeois-landlord regimes.[59] The very nature of the Socialist-Communist coalition, however, hindered his efforts to reach an understanding with the nationalities. The majority of the Socialists were more concerned about the defense of Hungary's historical boundaries than with the spread of revolution to other countries and were, therefore, little inclined to appease non-Magyar sensibilities. Kun himself and his party, moreover, owed their position of power and even their mass support to those who believed that they as Communists could gain the help of Soviet Russia and with it successfully defend the territorial integrity of the homeland.[60]

Rumanian Communists were also partly responsible for the strained relations with their Hungarian comrades. Their own coalition with the Internationalists had been marked by continual bickering over policy and tactics and by arrests of one faction by another.[61] They had also failed to serve the Soviet Republic by winning wide support for it among Rumanian peasants and workers in either Transylvania or Hungary. The five thousand Rumanian workers in Budapest and the surrounding mining centers, who could have formed the nucleus of a strong, class-conscious party, were alienated by the nationalism of Hungarian Socialists

---

[59] Tökés, *op. cit.*, p. 144.

[60] See the discussion of the nationality question in the Hungarian Soviet Republic in János M. Bak, "Die Diskussion um die Räterepublik in Ungarn 1919," *Jahrbücher für Geschichte Osteuropas*, N.F., XIV:4 (1966), 572–573.

[61] *Revoluţia Socială*, June 12, 1919.

and, particularly, by the inability of the government to improve their living and working conditions. In spite of repeated exhortations by party leaders, few workers came forward to join party organizations or the Rumanian revolutionary battalion which was supposed to assist the Hungarian Red Army in liberating Transylvania. Their lack of enthusiasm became so embarrassing that a party-sponsored Committee of Action in Budapest felt it necessary to threaten "drastic measures" against all workers who refused to join the Rumanian Communist movement.[62]

The crisis in Rumanian-Hungarian party relations came to a head on June 8 and 9, at a conference of Rumanian Communists in Budapest.[63] At the public session on the first day the course of revolution in Hungary was reviewed in general terms and on the whole favorably. The loudest praise, however, was reserved for Soviet Russia, which, according to Sava Demian Strengar, a leader of the pro-Hungarian wing of the party, "had taught us proletarians of Hungary the ABC's of revolution."

The atmosphere was different on the following day, when at a closed session party leaders candidly discussed the differences within their own ranks and with their Hungarian comrades. They were anxious to clarify their position on several major issues of party organization and responsibility before the congress of the Hungarian Socialist-Communist party on June 12–13 and the Congress of Councils on June 14–23. They had various grievances, but all were essentially national in origin. The delegates complained that Magyar chauvinism had not yet disappeared from the Socialist movement in Hungary and that they as Rumanians were

---

[62] *Ibid.,* June 1, 1919.
[63] What took place is described in detail in *Revolutia Sociala,* June 12, 1919.

continually subjected to discrimination. They accused the
Social Democrats in particular of seeking only the survival
of historical Hungary and of adhering to the formula *nem
nem soha*. The latter, they argued, had proclaimed the dictatorship of the proletariat not out of conviction but because
the actions of the Entente had frightened them into it.
Consequently, there was no place for them as Rumanians or
Socialists in a party that refused to respect the equality of all
Socialists regardless of nationality; although Hungarian
Communists who had been in Russia—"true Communists"
in the eyes of the Rumanians—recognized that this situation
existed, they had not taken appropriate action to correct it.
Perhaps, one delegate suggested, the Rumanians should consult with the German, Slovak, Serb, and Czech Communist
groups in order to devise a common plan to action to obtain
the recognition they deserved. If Hungary did not become a
true Bolshevik state, then they should refuse to accept any
other program except that of the Russian Bolsheviks, which,
they were convinced, offered the nationalities the greatest
possible freedom to develop. Russia had become for them,
as George Avramescu, the former editor of *Glasul Poporului*, put it, their "moral guarantee."

The majority of the delegates were clearly anxious to
maintain the national identity of their party, for they had
assigned it an important revolutionary task—the administration of Transylvania and other Rumanian-inhabited
areas as soon as they had been cleared of Rumanian troops.
They insisted, therefore, that the Rumanian Communist
organization be treated as an equal by the Hungarian Communist party and be allowed to manage its own affairs without outside interference. In particular, there should be no
repetition of what had occurred in Oradea in April just before its occupation by the Rumanian army when a delegate
from the central government in Budapest, contrary to Kun's

earlier promises about autonomy, summarily dissolved the Rumanian Consiliu Dirigent, the party's chief governing body. The Rumanians also demanded that the Hungarian Communist party provide more material support for their cause—a separate headquarters and meeting hall, new editorial offices for *Revoluția Socială*, a printing house where they could publish their own books and pamphlets destined for Transylvania, the Banat, and Rumania, and enough money for propagandists who were sent to these areas to enable them to finance pro-Communist newspapers and establish viable Communist organizations.

At the close of the conference a resolution embodying all these proposals was adopted and a delegation chosen to bring it before the central committee of the Hungarian Communist party. A second resolution urging the establishment of a federated republic in Hungary according to the model provided in the constitution of the Russian republic was also approved and forwarded to the Congress of Councils.

At the congress of the Hungarian Socialist-Communist party a few days later, Strengar, the Rumanian representative, observing that the Socialists had generally ignored Rumanian interests, demanded for his party not only the opportunity to deliberate but the right to make decisions as well and to have adequate representation in the highest councils of the Hungarian working-class movement.[64] No action on these requests was taken in the public session of the congress, but, judging from later events, negotiations in private between the two parties—of which we have no record, unfortunately—must have ended in an acceptable compromise. Rumanian Communists apparently agreed not to form a separate party, for by the middle of June they were

---

[64] *Ibid.*, June 22, 1919.

calling themselves the Rumanian Group of the Socialist-Communist Party of Hungary and were reaffirming their full support of the Soviet Republic. In return, they obtained the organizational autonomy and the control over the Rumanian working-class movement which had formed the heart of their program. At the end of June, undoubtedly inspired by the establishment of the Slovak Soviet Republic on the 16th of that month, they took the next logical step by proclaiming a Rumanian Soviet Republic and appealed to Rumanian workers to create a corps of agitators and a Rumanian Red Army with which to make it a reality. Although they announced simultaneously their intention of remaining within a Hungarian federated republic, their long-range goal was to establish a separate state ecompassing all lands inhabited by Rumanians, including the old kingdom and Bessarabia.[65] They denounced both the government in Bucharest and the Consiliu Dirigent in Sibiu and urged Rumanian workers and peasants to replace them with a dictatorship of the proletariat. Nevertheless, in spite of the substantial concessions to Rumanian national feeling which they had won and a renewed propaganda effort, there was little increase in worker participation in their movement.[66] The party apparatus itself disintegrated and its members scattered when the Hungarian Soviet Republic collapsed on August 1 and Rumanian troops occupied Budapest a few days later.

During the crisis in the Rumanian revolutionary movement in Hungary, the Social Democratic party in Sibiu was busy adapting itself to the new circumstances created by the union of Transylvania with Rumania. Its advocacy of na-

---

[65] *Ibid.*, June 29, 1919.
[66] *Ibid.*, July 17, 1919.

tional self-determination for the Rumanian people and its moderation on social questions had remained unchanged.

The attitude of party leaders toward the Hungarian Soviet Republic was at first hostile; they regarded it as a device to ensure the preservation of Hungary's historical boundaries and its leaders as "political charlatans." They reiterated their belief that Hungarian Socialists and Communists were engaged in a desperate gamble with socialist principles, inasmuch as the objective conditions for the transition to communism had not yet developed.[67] Nevertheless, they objected strongly to the Rumanian government's refusal to settle its differences with the Soviet Republic around a conference table rather than by force of arms. It seemed to them that Béla Kun represented the will of the Magyar people as well as the spirit of democracy and social justice, which they regarded as the hallmarks of the new age.[68] They could not understand why the Rumanian government refused to recognize him, for they took at face value his disavowal of a policy based upon the defense of Hungary's territorial integrity, and warned that the conservative regime which it sought to impose upon the Magyar people against their will was nationalistic and certain to become irredentist. Rumania, they believed, had a far better chance of protecting its new frontiers and living at peace with a Hungary governed by Kun rather than a Károlyi or some other count as its leader and decried their government's willingness to serve as the gendarme of Europe.[69] Their views, however, carried little weight with Rumanian political leaders, who ordered a final assault on the Hungarian Soviet Repblic, which began on July 24 and culminated in the capture of Budapest on August 4.

---

[67] *Adevărul,* March 17–30, 1919.

[68] *Ibid.,* July 13, 1919.

[69] *Ibid.,* June 29, 1919.

The failure of the Hungarian Soviet Republic to obtain the support of more than a handful of Rumanian Socialists must be attributed primarily to the latter's strong national feeling and belief that socialism could develop most effectively within the framework of the national state. The Hungarian Socialists and Communists who created the Soviet Republic inherited the nationality problem from their predecessors, and the persistence of Magyar nationalism in the Socialist-Communist coalition frustrated attempts to reach an understanding with the majority of Rumanian Socialists. Even those Rumanian revolutionaries who had allied themselves with the Soviet Republic could offer no other solution to the nationality problem than the creation, ultimately, of an independent soviet republic based upon nationality, and, when it appeared that their wishes were to be ignored, they appealed beyond the borders of Hungary to Bolshevik Russia. In the final analysis, whatever concessions the leadership of the Hungarian Soviet Republic might have made to the Rumanian Socialists—moderates or revolutionaries—it could have satisfied them only by recognizing their right of secession.

5

Austria's Geistesaristokraten and the Hungarian Revolution of 1919

William B. Slottman

THE Cisleithania's subjects of the Austrian empire had always been in danger of being upstaged by their more colorful and dynamic Hungarian neighbors.[1] From the moment of the conclusion of the *Ausgleich* of 1867 the Hungarians had revealed an increasing tendency to affront Austrian feelings of pride and precedence. Even the collapse of dualism in October 1918 brought no discernible relief, for in the weeks and months that followed the Hungarians did it again: they went far beyond the Austrians in experiencing the full gamut of revolution and civil war. The Austrians, to be sure, had put an end to the Habsburg monarchy by proclaiming a republic, and no one could deny that there had been difficult moments in the first weeks and months of the new republic, but this was nothing when compared with what was happening in Budapest and in the Hungarian countryside at the same time.

---

[1] This chapter owes much to the inspiration provided by Professor Walter Leitsch's study of a related problem, "Die Revolution der Intellektuellen: Die russische Oktoberrevolution und ihr Echo in Österreich," *Österreichische Osthefte*, X (January 1968), 1–14.

Carl Burckhardt, who had just arrived in the capital of the newly established German-Austria, failed to discover any signs that a revolution had taken place in this part of the old monarchy. There was nothing that could possibly remind a thoughtful Swiss observer of the zeal of the English Puritans, of the French Revolution with its guillotine "beating time," or of that "demonic liberation of Asiatic forces" which he associated with the recent Russian Revolution. As he put it,

> What happened there had nothing of the great convulsion about it. It was rather a weary, half-reluctant drift from one state of affairs to another, which in its turn would have no claim to permanence. There was something almost stealthy about the manner in which its sinister qualities did not thrust themselves forward in a violent way but rather lingered colorlessly in the background, rather like the horizon on November afternoons as it met the plains on which Vienna and Austria had so often acted as the West's front line of defence against the East.[2]

The Austrians may have been spared great cataclysm, but they were spared little else. Lack of food, malnutrition, disease—all the cumulative effect of years of war and blockade, and, in addition, a sudden and irrevocable loss of that ground upon which most Austrians had built their existence. For, unlike their jubilant neighbors in other parts of the erstwhile Habsburg monarchy, they could not rejoice at the end of foreign control and of Habsburg oppression but had to begin to reckon with the indisputable fact that they were now condemned to live their lives in a small, impoverished, and unstable state, in an Austria that had nothing great about it but of which it could be truly said

2 Carl J. Burckhardt, "Erinnerungen an Wien 1918–1919," *Begegnungen* (Zürich: Manesse, 1958), pp. 58–59.

that it was that (in Clemenceau's inspired phrase) *"qui reste."*

How did one come to terms with the loss of a country, with the brutal fact that the old Austria had simply ceased to exist? The question so troubled a young and promising journalist, Ernst Lothar, that he suffered from it in an almost physical way. But he had the hope of finding an answer to his question, for he had had the happy inspiration of discussing it with the one man in Vienna, in Rump Austria, who might be able to provide some consolation: Sigmund Freud. Lothar had written a flattering piece on the great psychoanalyst for his paper, and Freud had indicated his gratitude for the article. This provided an entree, and Lothar simply assumed that the man whose "X-ray eyes" were known to reveal the most profound secrets of the human soul would have no difficulty in diagnosing and curing the disease that was produced by the loss of one's country.[3]

Freud's waiting room on the Berggasse did not inspire much confidence when Lothar visited it; it looked for all the world like the waiting room of any Austrian physician. And Freud, too, when the patient had been announced and had taken a seat in his study, was not receptive at the start of the discussion. He acted as if Lothar had come to see him like any other patient in his field of medicine, and some time passed before he began to understand that Lothar's difficulty transcended the usual range of his medical experience. The first response, once it was clear what was at issue here, was predictable: he reminded Lothar of the biological fact that the mother, the analogue for country, customarily died before her children. There was the addi-

---

[3] For Lothar's account of this visit see his autobiography, *Das Wunder des Überlebens: Erinnerungen und Ergebnisse (Ausgewählte Werke)*, (Wien: Paul Zsolnay, 1961), V, 33–37.

tional biological fact that human beings have a built-in tendency to delude themselves in order to survive. Perhaps Herr Lothar had been guilty of such self-delusion and found himself now in mourning for an Austria that had never really existed.

Lothar was not to be so easily consoled nor was he to allow his deep attachment to the old Austria to be reduced to the level of an illusion. This made him all the more anxious to express his faith in Austria and to indicate how deeply he felt the loss of the "mother." Freud responded to this statement of faith by becoming suddenly communicative about himself in an effort to show that Lothar was not alone in his powerful sense of loss. Freud reminded Lothar that he had also come from Moravia and that he was quite as attached to Vienna, to Austria, even though he had better reason for knowing the darker side of that world. Reaching into his desk he produced some notes which he had jotted down on November 11, 1918, the day on which the death certificate of the old Austria had been officially signed, and without any comment he read them as his own reflections written under the impact of the event:

> Austria-Hungary has ceased to exist. I have no wish to live anywhere else. Emigration does not exist as a possibility for me. I shall convince myself that it is the whole body.[4]

Lothar left Freud's office with the chill consolation that one of the greatest living Austrians was no stranger to the pain he felt so keenly. The death throes of the Habsburg monarchy had indeed registered on the preternaturally sensitive and probing mind of Sigmund Freud, but they

---

[4] "Österreich-Ungarn ist nicht mehr. Anderswo möchte ich nicht leben. Emigration kommt für mich nicht in Frage. Ich werde mit dem Torso weiterleben und mir einbilden, dass es das Ganze ist," *ibid.*, 37.

had produced a most uncharacteristic reaction. For the great enemy of illusion, the student of the human psyche who so often called his contemporaries to a life that accepted reality without evasion or afterthought, was revealed in this instance to be preaching the necessity of living with an illusion in order to be able to survive spiritually in the debris of the Monarchy.

Lothar's meeting with Freud is of interest for the light it throws on a figure of Freud's stature reacting to a great event of this kind; it also helps to establish the mood which existed in Vienna in the last days of 1918, the mood that had so little of the traditional revolutionary tone about it. Lothar's meeting with Freud provides a fascinating perspective, too, on the manner in which Austria's most gifted men and women were responding in a critical time not just to Austria's demise but to all of the forces of twentieth-century history whose workings had been suddenly revealed at that time. A part of that total climate of events and ideas was the developing revolutionary movement in Hungary, and it may be interesting to inquire what these Austrian *Geistesaristokraten,* these magnates in the arts and letters, had to say about the establishment of the Hungarian Soviet Republic. What did the dramatic travail of Hungary in that period do to alter or to reinforce their customary views of the way of the world in Central Europe? Perhaps such an inquiry is too blatantly the product of a curiosity that should be restrained, perhaps it is condemned to defeat from the start because these great men were not inclined to indulge in elaborate comment on Hungary and its Soviet Republic. Genius such as theirs was unlikely to produce the instantaneous wisdom that makes for good newspaper copy or for quotable material in a study of the interaction of the Austrian mind and Hungarian revolution. Yet in their own inimitable way they had important things to say about events and personalities a little more than two hundred kilometers away and in so doing they reveal much about their own grasp of a political form that was to play an increasingly influential role in the life of nations just released from the "prison of peoples." Perhaps such reflecting as they did in the midst of the most trying physical and psychological conditions may have the useful effect of righting the balance in some degree between Austrians and Hungarians. For if Hungary still led the competition in the dimension of political event, Austrian genius might still save the day for Austria by substituting critical awareness and analysis for the crudity of deeds done in the revolutionary cause.

Vienna at the turn of the century had witnessed an explosion of genius second to none.[5] The names associated with that not entirely expected triumph are too well known to be listed. Music, theater, poetry, philosophy, architecture, journalism that was undeniably great literature, medicine, physics—every major human concern had been touched by the creative spirit of a society in the advanced stages of dissolution. Every learned discipline followed suit at some respectable distance by producing a "Viennese school" as if to drive the point home beyond a doubt. Much of this grandeur was not public knowledge at the time, but enough of it had surfaced to convince even the skeptical that intellectual and artistic stagnation was not pursuing Europe's "middle kingdom" to its grave. The world of the coffee house celebrated here its undeniable apotheosis, and a style of life was fashioned that would in time penetrate to the remotest corners of the world. Vienna had come into its own without really knowing why, and all of the intensity, the clash of personalities and the existence of small groups

---

[5] For a recent appreciation of this "cultural efflorescence," see Frank Field, *The Last Days of Mankind: Karl Kraus and His Vienna* (London: Macmillan, 1967), ix.

of kindred spirits, the wit and the woe—all these were to become important elements in European culture and by a process of extrapolation themes in humanity's growth in self-awareness. The figures who peopled the stage of that ineffably Viennese *Welttheater* were suddenly playing on a greater stage, one that lived up to the pretensions of universality which had always existed there.

At the heart of this achievement were thirty or forty individuals who were unique and yet possessed of distinct common goals. They shared a background dominated by security and material ease; they had revealed their gifts in a score of the monarchy's gymnasiums and universities; they had been quick to discover that they lived in a *Wert-Vakuum,* in a setting whose moral standards were more and more nonexistent.[6] This loss of ethical substance was reflected in innumerable ways by the society in which they lived: strident politics, corrupt journalism, eclecticism in art, an academic philosophy that had been eroded from within. The list was long, and it could not fail to move them to a courageous and sometimes misunderstood effort to replace the tarnished values of a declining liberal culture with ideals and principles that reflected a more nuanced and successful view of the nature of man and society. This drive toward authenticity and the perfection of new forms of art and discourse and scientific inquiry required that the first stage of the new development be dominated by the removal of the debris of the dead culture. Philistinism of both the official and unofficial varieties stood in the way, and a whole younger generation rebelled against its emptiness, its mediocrity.[7] The struggle to accustom Austrians to think and to

---

[6] For Hermann Broch's classical discussion of this *Wert-Vakuum* see his extended study of Hofmannsthal and his times, *Dichten und Erkennen: Essays* (Zürich: Rhein, 1955), I, 43–181, especially pp. 66–95.

[7] Paul Stefan-Gruenfeldt, *Das Grab in Wien; eine Chronik 1903–1911* (Berlin: E. Reiss, 1913).

feel in ever new and more exciting ways was intense, and for a long time had to be conducted almost as guerrilla warfare. But by the fall of 1918 there were signs that this fight at least had been successful and that if Austria was fated to disappear as a great community of destiny and history it was also bound to survive as a permanent acquisition of the human spirit.

For all the apparent novelty and strangeness of the movement, it did not fail to reveal its Austrian origins. The emphasis on the aesthetic dimension of experience, the sensibility that still had some filial ties with Baroque Catholicism, the preservation in a spiritualized way of aristocratic values—all of this made it possible to describe these men of genius in Robert Musil's somewhat ironic way as *Geistesaristokraten,* as lifelong members of a *Herrenhaus* designed for aristocrats not of blood but of the spirit.[8]

Austria was no stranger to such an aristocracy, for all its modern history had witnessed attempts to supplement the traditional nobility which seemed so bereft of creative imagination and political talent with an *Adel des Geistes,* an order of men who would bring their talent to the service of the humane ideals that lingered in the mentality of the state of Joseph II.[9] Members of the clergy, the bureaucracy, the officer corps had served Austria well in this capacity, and if their service had often been overlooked or forgotten it had been a sign that even Austria could attract talent to

---

8 Robert Musil, "Monolog eines Geistesaristokraten," *Tagebücher, Aphorismen, Essays und Reden,* ed. A. Frisé (Hamburg: Rowohlt, 1955), pp. 844–846.

9 I discussed the tradition of an *Adel des Geistes* in the Habsburg Monarchy at the beginning of the nineteenth century in an unpublished paper, "The Aristocracy of Moral Worth," which was delivered at the annual meeting of the American Historical Association in San Francisco, December 28, 1965.

its cause and provide some ethical foundation for its day-to-day operations as a political entity. With the advance of modernization in Austrian society this "nobility" had moved beyond the circumscribed worlds of the parish church and the drill field and had taken on most of the characteristics of the intelligentsias of Western Europe with the understandable admixture of Austrian insouciance.

The members of this caste did not incline by nature to political activity or to musing on the state of politics. The internal history of Cisleithania did not inspire much confidence in political life, and men of intelligence more and more turned from a contemplation of that institutionalized chaos to more sublime undertakings. The progress or lack of it in the other half of the dual monarchy had even less chance of inspiring confidence, and here even men of great talent could not fail to be influenced in some degree by the notions that were current in Austria about Hungary and things Hungarian. Even when they tried to go beyond the level of popular prejudice they were only confronted by newspaper accounts that did more to reflect the ideological commitments and the official subsidies received by the publishers than to provide an accurate and intelligible account of Hungarian public life.

At the lowest level of understanding Austrians tended to look upon Hungary and Hungarians with a wonderful mixture of envy, ignorance, misplaced enthusiasm, and a large measure of contempt.[10] Envy was explicable enough in terms of Hungary's impressive showing since 1867 as the "junior partner" in the fine old firm had moved to a place of leadership. The ignorance was less forgivable. It seemed

---

[10] In the absence of any dependable literature on the image of Hungarians in Austria in the last years of dualism I have had to be impressionistic.

as if the long-standing association with the kingdom of St. Stephen had done little to provide the average Austrian with information on his Hungarian neighbor; in this instance proximity had not been the direct cause of affection or of familiarity with Hungarian problems. The Viennese did not immediately think of Budapest in making plans for trips or arranging for vacations; the thrust of his sensibility was in a westerly direction. Hungary appeared only fitfully there; it did not have the power of distracting the best intentioned of Austrians for long, as Italy, Germany, France, even England reasserted their influence.

The Magyar, it was true, did play his apparently providential role as one of the more colorful elements of the monarchy's mosaic of peoples, and a *Geistesaristokrat* like Joseph Roth was to contribute to the elaboration of this conception of Hungary pretty much in the manner of a Strauss whose *Fledermaus* had not failed to have its brief fiery Hungarian interlude:

> Klänge der Heimat,
> Ihr weckt mir das Sehnen,
> Rufet die Tränen,
> Ins Auge mir.
> Wenn ich euch höre,
> Ihr heimischen Lieder,
> Zieht mich's wieder,
> Mein Ungarland, zu dir.
>
> . . . .
>
> Feuer, Lebenslust,
> Schwellt echte Ungarbrust. . . .
> Hei, zum Tanze schnell,
> Czardas tönt so hell.[11]

---

[11] The gypsies of the puszta take their place among Joseph Roth's colorful collection of the peoples of the Austro-Hungarian monarchy.

Rosalinde was acting according to plan in expressing sentiments of this kind; it was almost as if a special form of
kitsch served its usual function of substituting for real
thought and empathy.

This refusal to go deeper and to confront Hungary
and Hungarians at a somewhat more profound level could
be traced in part to perennial Austrian irritation with
Hungarian politics, particularly as it had some bearing on
the fate of Austrians. The chief villain in this scenario was
not the Hungarian magnate but the typical member of
the Hungarian gentry—chauvinistic, legalistic, and essentially provincial. The magnates had had the inspired good
taste of developing an enthusiasm for Viennese ways and
for the political tie with Austria; their lesser brethen in
the Hungarian political nation had vegetated all the while
with incalculable adverse effects on the internal consistency
and the external prestige of the dual monarchy. Austrians
could not forget that these hillbillies were a part of the
"East" and that their spiritual world was that of the Balkans
rather than of Central Europe. Dissatisfication joined here
with an easy contempt for the *Ostleute* who seemed per-
petually beyond the pale.

Such attitudes, composed of a wide range of reflex
actions and defense mechanisms, did not exhaust the possi-
bilities in the contacts of Austria and Hungary. Room had
to be left for occasional snippets of information that passed
for Austrian understanding of the latest developments in
Hungary. It was somewhat mysterious, this mixture of fact
and rumor that provided even the most perceptive Austrians
with a basis for analysis and, eventually, judgment of the

See, for example, a passage in *Die Kapuzinergruft* in *Werke in Drei
Bänden* (Köln-Berlin: Kiepenheuer and Witsch, 1956), I, 357. I have
quoted from the text of *Die Fledermaus* that accompanies the London
recording, X 5588, p. 15.

Hungarian revolution of 1919—above all in the period
of the Kun regime. The self-imposed isolation which was
allowed to settle in on Hungary did not help matters,
though even this isolation was pierced by the reports, however tendentious, of travelers and refugees from Bolshevism.
The articles filed by reporters and the telephone calls from
the Hungarian capital might cease, but still the raw material
managed somehow to make its way to a Viennese journal-
istic establishment that seemed uncertain how it would use
such information.

The journals that represented a clear political option,
and here one thinks immediately of the Christian Socialist
Reichspost and the Social Democratic *Arbeiter-Zeitung,*
could not accept what they received without some degree
of rearrangement no matter how genteel and tentative it
might be. The *Reichspost* could not restrain itself on the
whole, and its reporting of the Hungarian revolution proved
so vitriolic that it aroused the ire of Viennese radicals to
the point of an outright attack on the offices of the paper.[11]
If it had not been for the timely intervention of more
moderate elements Dr. Friedrich Funder, the editor, and
his staff might have experienced the full range of an aroused
mob. The tradition of Karl Lueger was too strong here to
be overcome in a few weeks; his antipathy to Budapest and
to its Jewish community persisted even under the radically
different circumstances of 1919. The report that a large
number of Jews held positions of importance in the Béla
Kun regime did nothing to allow for a more nuanced view
of Hungarian developments.

The Social Democrats with their *Arbeiter-Zeitung* and
their distinguished theoretical journal *Der Kampf* might

---

[12] Friederich Funder, *Vom Gestern ins Heute: Aus dem Kaiserreich in
die Republik* (Wien: Herold, 1953), pp. 623–624.

have been particularly useful to Austrian intellectuals at a juncture when Marxism had entered upon an outright, even flamboyant, revolutionary phase—across the border.[13] But for all their awareness of what might be happening in Hungary, these Social Democrats, these Austromarxists, had a tremendous interest in preventing the same thing from happening at home. Coverage of the Kun regime, then, was detailed enough and without the stridency of the *Reichspost*, but there was evidence that tactics played a role in the picture the loyal party members were to receive of the fraternal effort of Hungarian Social Democrats and Communists. At times an uneasy silence could be observed (this was especially true of *Der Kampf*), and at other times a refusal to face realities that seemed strangely out of place for orthodox Marxists in a time of great revolutionary change. Perhaps it was just another instance of the Austrian party's tendency to talk tough and to act moderately, though there was evidence, too, that the leadership—gifted men like Otto Bauer, Karl Renner, Friedrich Adler, and Max Adler, the Social Democratic delegation in the *Herrenhaus* of the spirit—had reasons for being unenthusiastic about the apparent advances—in both Hungary and Russia. At least they realized that Austria had less room to maneuver at that time; the *Entente* dominated Austria in a way he did not dominate Hungary.

This left our putative observer in the most advanced circles of Austrian thought with a paper like the *Neue Freie Presse*, which for all its service of the upper middle class ideal, its connivance with government policy under the dual monarchy, its faint aura of corruption (*pace* Karl Kraus),

[13] Alfred D. Low, "The First Austrian Republic and Soviet Hungary," *Journal of Central European Affairs*, XX:1 (April 1960), 174–203, discusses the reactions of Austrian Social Democrats and of the *Arbeiter-Zeitung* at some length.

represented the best that one could do in ascertaining the real state of affairs in Hungary. The *Neue Freie Presse* even at a time of the deescalation of Austrian involvement in what had once been a part of the Habsburg monarchy retained the format, the general cleverness, and the self-assurance of a great European daily. Even Karl Kraus had not been able to change that picture very much. In the first months of 1919 people inclined to be tolerant of the infrequent sins against the purity of the German language; at a time of general collapse and loss of direction it seemed a most minute offense. The *Presse* acted as if it were the *Times* of Austria, of an Austria pathetically reduced by policies it had once supported with enthusiasm.

In March 1919, its columns fairly tingled with up-to-the-minute reports from the Hungarian border and Budapest. The first reaction in the lead articles devoted to Hungary was automatic and without even the virtue of a moment's doubt: the events in Hungary were only the latest outrage for which the *Entente* must bear full responsibility. The triumph of Bolshevism in a country as bereft of capital and, by implication, of a developed industrial system, had to be understood in terms of external pressures; the Vy note had performed the chemical process of converting embittered Hungarian nationalism into extreme social radicalism, which was being carried, as the article said, to the "point of degeneration."[14]

This Olympian position by which both Austria and Hungary appeared to escape responsibility for what happened in either country did not endure for long. The *Neue Freie Presse* with a trace of *Schadenfreude* warned its readers that they must be aware of one fact that could not be overlooked "Bolshevism is at the gates of Vienna."[15] No

[14] *Neue Freie Presse*, March 22, 1919, p. 1.
[15] *Ibid.*, March 23, 1919, p. 1.

Austrian could overlook the obvious analogies with earlier appearances of Asiatic movements; one continued to live as if 1683 and the Turkish siege had happened a few months before. Yet in the midst of these most judicious alarums one positive "advantage" could not be overlooked; Austrians who had an interest in knowing what it was like to live under Bolshevism no longer needed to contemplate the long and difficult trip to Russia; they might now form their immediate impressions after a train ride of a few hours' duration.

This flurry of interest could not be sustained for too long, and it perished, as one might have foreseen, in the rush of bad news from Munich, Berlin, Prague, and Austria itself. Somehow Hungary could not hold the attention of Vienna's most important newspaper, but that should not cause surprise; it had never had any luck in this way with Austria itself. The complex relationships between the Kun regime and attempts at a Communist putsch on at least two occasions in Vienna did not add to the sum of general enlightenment; they only hardened the lines and allowed the advance of the Rumanian army upon Budapest to acquire the air of a crusade. Austrians could fear that they might be compelled to mimic revolution in Budapest, a threat that was unlikely to arouse much enthusiasm for communism in Hungary or in Austria, and this threat took on all the more credibility because Hungary in its turn lived according to the latest Russian political and social style:

> Budapest is rapidly becoming a Magyar Moscow. One follows all the recipes in the little Russian cookbook . . . with occasional addition of a little paprika as a sign of independence.[16]

---

16 *Ibid.*, April 23, 1919, p. 1.

The *Geistesaristokraten* were required to depend on sources such as these, full of the old prejudices and painfully anxious to acquire new ones, in forming their own highly charged impressions of the "Magyar Moscow." We do not know how many of these men performed such a task or what general impressions developed in this group. The year 1919 found the group's ranks thinned by death and diminished by the varying forms of internal exile.[17] Gustav Klimt and Egon Schiele had died the previous year, and Schiele's death on the last day of October was a symbol for the death of the monarchy at the same time—this even in the face of the variance between its tone and his artistic achievement. Peter Altenberg died at the beginning of 1919 and was spared the spectacle of a revolution in Hungary that might have provided an occasion for the display of his wonderfully wry and understated prose.

Other members of the group were too much involved in projects of their own to give much thought to Hungary and its revolution. Kokoschka, "der tolle Kokoschka", was living in Dresden, and his major interest appeared to be a doll which was manufactured for him and which had a celebrated arrival in the Saxon capital. Though some hardy spirits might take this to be the most apt comment of all on the political scene in Hungary and elsewhere, there seems to be no easy way of transmitting that phantasy in the baser frequencies of political commentary. Arnold Schönberg, Alban Berg, Anton Webern—they all felt an unexpected liberation from the dead hand of official philistinism and were dedicated to the work of the new musical society which they had just founded. Their letters were full of plans for the

---

[17] The roll call that follows does not pretend to be complete; it is based on biographies of the *Geistesaristokraten* as well as diaries and letters that discuss their activities in this period.

revolutionary change of music in Vienna and made no mention of a similar effort of a more egregiously political nature in Budapest. Ludwig Wittgenstein devoted himself as wholeheartedly to finding himself intellectually and spiritually; in the summer of 1919 he worked as an assistant gardener for the Augustinian canons at Klosterneuburg. Hugo von Hofmannsthal, dividing his time between his apartment in Vienna and his home in Rodaun, mourned the passing of the old Austria and the social and aesthetic order which it had represented; he, too, had no surplus of energy or interest to devote to any other theme.

Rilke was to have a personal contact with the revolutionary forces that pullulated through Central and Eastern Europe.[18] He encountered his "revolution" in Munich in November 1918. The event had made a fairly favorable impression on him; at least he had found himself not noticing some of the more folksy aspects of intense political meetings conducted in Munich's beer halls. These were "wonderful moments" as things were finally said in the open which had needed to be said for so long a time. Munich in the November days had little similarity to Budapest in the spring of 1919; the atmosphere was still too *bajuwarisch* for that, and it would require some time before political radicalism that could be compared with the best or worst of Hungarian communism would emerge. By that time Rilke had left Munich and had settled in Switzerland.

Some *Geistesaristokraten* had contacts of a sort with Hungary in revolution. Stefan Zweig, for example, returned home to Vienna (he passed the former emperor on his way into exile) and discovered there that his original plan to go to Hungary to secure a Hungarian divorce—the Hungar-

---

[18] Rainer Maria Rilke to Clara Rilke, Munich, November 7, 1918, *Briefe* (Wiesbaden: Insel, 1950), pp. 561–563.

ians having been more broadminded about such matters than the Austrians—would have to be abandoned in the face of the sudden change in the Hungarian government.[19]

Sigmund Freud surely regretted the loss of the food packages from Hungary which had been such a blessing during the last months of the war, but this privation was not to end his connection with Hungarian followers and their involvement in Hungarian politics. The advent of the Hungarian Soviet Republic brought with it official support for psycholanalysis; the two great movements had not yet come to a parting of the ways ideologically. And in the euphoria created by this new state of affairs there was thought for a time of shifting some of the activities of world Freudianism to Hungary, but Freud counseled men like Sándor Ferenczi, now a professor at the university, to assume a reserved position in regard to political developments. He told them that they might take such comfort as they could from the fact that psychoanalysis allowed them to get to the tragic heart of things, a form of knowledge impossible for most mortals. The collapse of the Hungarian Communist regime ended this brief chapter in Freud's life and in that of his movement, and those who had prospered briefly under Béla Kun now began to suffer as a result of the cultural backwardness and virulent anti-Semitism of the Horthy regime.[20]

In Innsbruck the circle which had grown up around Ludwig Ficker and his *Der Brenner*—men like Carl Dallago, Friedrich Ebner, and Theodor Haecker in Munich— could have turned events of this kind to good use by an analysis that was a dexterous mixture of a concern for re-

[19] Stefan Zweig, *The World of Yesterday: An Autobiography* (New York: Viking, 1943), pp. 283–285.
[20] For an account of Freud's contacts with his Hungarian disciples during the Hungarian Revolution, cf. Ernest Jones, *The Life and Work of Sigmund Freud* (New York: Basic, 1957), III, 3–17.

ligious values and an adherence to the existentialist tradition. The magazine began publishing again just at a time when such a reaction in depth would have been timely, but its articles were devoted to expounding on these themes rather than to discussing issues of the day. Only Carl Dallago broke this unofficial ban on the discussion of newsworthy questions by an article that discussed the relation of Christianity and the "social question." Admittedly the tone was at so high a level that historical phenomena had to seem remote and unreal. He pointed to the fact that socialism's weaknesses were now made manifest; it was a movement that was forced to seek refuge in force. On the one side it served as a cover for the further development of capitalism.

> On the other hand—actually the more honest and influential one—it becomes transformed into communism, the realization of the idea of equality, which is an anomaly in existence. Already these most progressive Socialists present themselves as Spartacists and wish to enforce the salvation of mankind through deeds of violence.[21]

The goal of equality, and not some internal necessity, was the force which drove this branch of socialism to murder and to plundering. Dallago's interest in contemporary politics derived from his all-consuming interest in restoring Christianity to the "religious dimension," and if this deprived his comments on communism (here the Spartacists might substitute for Hungarian Communists) of a degree of actuality he might be excused. Life in the Tyrol was hardly calculated to arouse passionate involvement in social experimentation in the Danubian plain.

Of all this stratum of Austrian cultural and intellectual

---

[21] From his "Das Christliche und Soziale," *Der Brenner,* VI:5, pp. 372–399.

life only three can be found who had something important
to say about the Hungarian revolution of 1919: Gustav Stolper, the gifted editor of the prestigious *Der Österreichische
Volkswirt*, Robert Musil, the novelist who was then on active service in the republic's equivalent of the Ministry of
War, and Karl Kraus, the idiosyncratic cultural giant of that
epoch who could not have passed up an opportunity to pass
judgment on the Hungarians even if he had wanted to do
so. In its own inimitable way that revolution had a way of
thrusting itself on a mind that managed to respond to almost
all chaotic impressions bombarding the Austrian sensibility
in 1919.

Stolper had a reputation as a shrewd commentator on
economic problems but on political ones as well, and he had
written movingly some years before on the need for the continued existence of the monarchy.[22] Now that it was gone he
could reexamine many of his assumptions without falling
prey to confusion or to wild oscillations in his thinking; he
would bring to his writing on Hungary the same intelligence, general information, and moderation which he
brought to the discussion of problems closer to home.

The first signs of his reaction to Hungarian "confu-
sions" were not particularly stimulating. Stolper reminded
his readers of the awesome legacy left by the Hungarian
policy that had denied much needed foodstuffs to Austrians
during the war. He could also not rid himself of the unfavor-
able impression created by the South Slav question—the
Lebensfrage of the Monarchy—which owed so much of its
lethal character to Hungarian hardheadedness. In January
1919, he could see some hope for a Danubian confederation
with Austria and Hungary leading the way, but he was

---

22 For Gustav Stolper's career see Toni Stolper, *Ein Leben in Brenn-
punkten unserer Zeit: Wien Berlin New York: Gustav Stolper 1888–
1947* (Tübingen: Rainer Wunderlich, 1960).

quick to admit that Michael Károlyi's pronouncements on that subject did not inspire him with much confidence; the Hungarians were too prone to use that notion as a device with which to secure the preservation of the territorial integrity of prewar Hungary. Now with Austria and Hungary both brought low, the Hungarians might be more amenable to reason. Yet once again, Károlyi was an obstacle to the rapprochement between Germans and Hungarians; his reputation as an outspoken critic of Wilhelminian Germany during the war ensured that he would not be the man to carry through such an *Anschluss.*[23]

It was not until the end of August that Stolper returned to a discussion in depth of the Hungarian revolution.[24] This was to be his final word if only because of the date on which his article appeared; it also revealed that his thinking had not changed much under the impact of Hungarian events. For him the finale of the Kun regime and its immediate consequences only served to remind Austrians of how foreign Hungary actually was. For with the fall from power of the traditional ruling class the amorphous nature of Hungarian society, a trait it shared with Balkan societies, had been crushingly revealed. Attempts to find a way out of the chaos had so far been unproductive. The Hungarian Social Democrats were particularly disappointing, and it was no great mistake on the part of Kun's conservative successors to treat them as a negligible quantity in Hungarian politics. One missed the clear record of achievement of the Austrian working class, and, as for Hungarian social democracy, it lacked leadership of the kind provided by Viktor Adler in Austria. The Communists, for all their evident weaknesses

---

[23] Gustav Stolper, "Donauföderation oder Grossdeutschland," *Der Österreichische Volkswirt,* XI:14 (1919), p. 3.

[24] "Die Ungarische Wirren," *Der Österreichische Volkswirt,* XI:48 (1919) pp. 905–906.

and failures, had been quite different from the *Hotelpolitiker of* Hungarian social democracy; these were men who knew where they were going and who had proceeded toward their goal in a single-minded way that left no room for second thoughts and for hesitations.

Stolper's conclusion was that all this was deeply, essentially foreign to the Austrian experience. As long as Kun had been in power, Hungarian communism had been a threat to German-Austria if only because it was the material representation of a powerful idea, but there was nothing now in Hungarian politics that represented a threat to the delicate balance in Austria. Even the most conservative element in the country—the German peasant of the Alpine *Länder*—had no tie to the newly established "Christian" politicians in Budapest any more than he had had with the "Jewish Communists." The German peasant had the good sense to realize just how little he had in common—with the East.

Musil's reflections began just when Stolper had brought his to a conclusion, and the novelist's interest was aroused not by the fall of Kun but by a long quotation he took from a speech of Horthy on his arrival in Budapest that was reported in the Viennese press. Musil noted in his entry of November 16, 1919: "Mirror of the times: An incisive event has taken place in the entry of Horthy's troops into Budapest; speeches were made not one word of which belongs to the present times." [25]

He was to return to this idea shortly thereafter when he embarked on a lengthy discussion of the extent to which Europe's political leaders had missed the significance of the demand for a new form of politics; they remained caught up in their viewpoint which was "nationalistic-etatist-conceived in the light of *Realpolitik*." Wilson's speeches, which had

---

[25] Robert Musil, Tagebuch, Heft 9, in *Tagebücher*, p. 216.

produced so amazing a response from Europeans generally, had had little chance of being understood by such a mentality. "The same inability to free oneself from the costumes of the past can be seen in contemporary Hungary and in the speech of Horthy which I noted down."[26]

Musil went on to say that there could be no doubt that conservative forces had brought the world much misfortune. The same could be said for the opposite extreme, though here he excepted Bolshevism for a moment because it was so often maligned and because the effort to seek enlightenment on this subject had been insufficient. But he had no such reluctance to speak about its Hungarian counterpart which had brought to the surface and to power so much "filth, shame, corruption, etc." The Hungarian case and the murder of the hostages in Munich established a picture of revolution and of the revolutionary type that was gaining more and more in internal plausibility. The revolutionary was the man "who could fly but could not walk, who swam under the water but could not breathe in the open air."

For Musil the truly creative response to political problems came from men whose decisions were consciously made in the presence of life and of death; the extremist, on the other hand, burned at one moment for the inviolability of each hair on a human face, while in another he condemned thousands to death without batting an eye. Yet for all this the revolutionary, who could only mimic the truly creative personality, was a social necessity as much a part of the historical process as war and social injustice. He was unable to carry projects through to fulfillment though he was capable of inaugurating them. It was the conservative man who had to finish the work, and it was on him that the guilt rested finally rather than on the revolutionary.

Revolution and counterrevolution in Hungary had

---

[26] *Ibid.*, pp. 219–221.

been able to arouse Musil's interest to a point where it became a part of his thinking about the roles of revolutionary and conservative forces. He had been careful to distribute blame on both sides and yet there was no doubt at all that he felt the sterility of the avowed conservatives in Hungary much more keenly than he did the excesses of the Hungarian Soviet Republic. The obvious inability of men like Horthy to understand what had taken place and to produce a positive achievement could only be taken by Musil to be a part of the greater and more general refusal to respond to the needs of a critical period in European history.

When he had meditated on Horthy's speech, he had made reference to Karl Kraus. It was a simple enough question as where Kraus would stay: *Wo wird Karl Kraus bleiben?* This enigmatic inquiry by a man who was not enthusiastic about Kraus and his public image brings us to a discussion of how Kraus, acting in his customary role as the unofficial conscience of Austria, viewed the Hungarian revolution. The end of the monarchy had not put an end to Kraus' effectiveness as a public figure; the numbers of *Die Fackel* were awaited with even more anticipation. In the chaotic situation immediately after the war a man who spoke with such prophetic certainty was bound to have an influence on men who felt themselves to be lost. He was also bound to arouse resentment in quarters which did not share his views of the world. As Kraus continued to blame the old regime for the depressing state of affairs brought about by the Soviet Republic, found that he was being accused of favoring revolution and Bolshevism. It was characteristic of the man that he defended himself by brilliant attacks upon those who were responsible for the war and its aftermath. One of the short but effective instances of this polemic was to provide Kraus with a platform for the discussion of the early stages of the Hungarian revolution, that is before the establishment of the Kun regime.

The last scene of the last act of Kraus's *Die letzten Tage der Menschheit* includes a brief and depressing appearance of a Hungarian staff officer by the name of Géza von Lakkati de Némesfalva et Kutjafelegfaluszég, and Karl Kraus remembered this figure when he delivered one of his public readings on January 1, 1919.[27] The title of the selection was the name of the Hungarian officer, and the name itself was sufficient to evoke a picture of that remote and frightening world of Hussar officers with names which defied pronunciation. Kraus admitted that he had taken pains with the production of that name, for only if one found the right mixture could one be certain of revealing the truly nauseating quality of a whole epoch. "Monsters" like Géza von Lakkati had not received the punishment they deserved in Hungary; they and their German equivalents appeared certain to return to power thanks to their ability to manipulate the specter of Bolshevism. In Kraus's mind, "Bolshevism is not merely the attempt to drive the devil out with the aid of Beelzebub it was also the certainty that he would return by the other door." The sabre-rattling of a Hungarian officer, who though a fictional character had in many minds undeniable claims to authenticity, troubled Kraus most, and he could not but believe that any revolution which grew out of such a milieu would be as squalid as that which had produced it.

The figure of Géza von Lakkati was not to dominate all of Kraus's contacts with Hungarian affairs. In the wake of the collapse of the Soviet Republic Vienna was flooded with refugees from Hungary, and one of them rose to great prominence as a journalist in Vienna. This was Imre Békessy, the man who more than anyone else was to become the great *bête noire* of Kraus in the years that followed. Békessy's

---

[27] Karl Kraus, *Die letzten Tage der Menschheit* in *Werke,* ed. Heinrich Fischer (München: Kösel, 1957), V, 701–702; "Géza von Lakkati de Némesfalva et Kutjafelegfaluszég," *Die Fackel,* XXI:521–530 (January 1920), 161–164.

very success in the changing world of Viennese yellow journalism was such that he quickly earned himself a special place of dishonor in the Krausian demonology.[28] Reports from Budapest told of a police record, of an attempt to make personal advantage out of the various stages in the Hungarian revolution—now working against the Communists, now working with them, now working against them again when the Kun regime collapsed. Békessy's presence in Vienna became intolerable for Kraus, and in *Die Fackel* the whole ethical problem raised by the success and influence of such a man was discussed with what some might feel to be obsessive detail. In August 1926, Kraus could report with satisfaction that the "scoundrel" (*Schuft*) was no longer in Austria. In the course of this long and finally successful campaign to remove Békessy from the scene Kraus had to deal, if only tangentially, with the atmosphere that was responsible for the emergence of so ambiguous a figure. Hungary had its Géza von Lakkati; it also had to bear the guilt for an Imre Békessy. Something of the flavor of Kraus at work on Békessy and on Budapest can be discerned in a sentence like this: "Welche Macht doch so ein Spitzbub, der's vom Pester Kriegswurstschieber und Menschenfleischschinder bis zum Diktator der geistigen Prostitution Wiens bringen konnte —welche Macht er doch selbst über mich hat." [29]

This was the extent of the reaction of the Austrian *Geistesaristokraten* to our "public opinion poll" on the Hungarian revolution. The results were more interesting than one might have been led to expect. The grandees of the

---

[28] Field, *op. cit.*, pp. 153–169; for Gustav Stolper's struggle against Békessy, see Stolper, *op. cit.*, pp. 151–158.

[29] Karl Kraus, "Die Stunde des Todes," *Die Fackel,* XXVIII:732–734 (Mitte August 1926), 5.

spirit had paused for some moments in their creative lives to ponder the meaning of revolution Hungarian-style. Their response had been personal and not without a crude admixture of popular prejudice and ignorance of things Hungarian, yet the great moral concern and the sense that a new world was in the process of formation had been there as well. From such a perspective the Hungarian revolution took on a slightly different appearance than that which was prevalent in the popular press. Here there was no wild and hasty adverse judgment of Hungarian communism but a patent desire to understand it before a final judgment was made. The full force of their disappointment with the direction of affairs in Hungary had been vented, not on the commissars, but on the conservative forces that had replaced them. This was the significance of the figure of Géza von Lakkati; this was the meaning of Musil's careful study of a speech of Admiral Horthy. The radicals in a revolutionary situation were less responsible for what happened at such a time than the forces which had brought about a war which had in its turn led to civil war and revolution.

In producing an analysis of this kind Austrian genius had not managed to make up for the inferiority other Austrians might feel in the presence of Hungarian activism in the political sphere. Two figures had been added to the repertoire of Hungarians on the Austrian stage—the swaggering hussar officer and the corrupt journalist. The endurance and credibility of such figures depended in part on the gifts of a Kraus and not on the intrinsic merits of the case. The *Geistesaristokraten* had stopped short of a complete analysis for a variety of reasons. It was not after all their stock in trade. It may well have been partly due to the fact that even in an unguarded moment like this they were being loyal to the aristocratic values of their "class." What surely did figure here in the limits imposed on their understanding of the Hungarian revolution was the growing gap between *Geist* and *Politik*, between a dimension in which they were at home and another that had taken on a threatening and uncertain life of its own that it could not be compressed even with the greatest talent into one final, manageable formula.

6

The Hungarian Soviet
and International Communism

Richard Löwenthal

THE following thoughts which I, not a specialist on Hungary, would like to put forward, discuss the character of the Hungarian revolution of 1918–1919, and the consequences of this revolution for the international Communist movement.[1] To do so makes it necessary to start with a basic incongruity that existed between the realities of the general European situation and the Communist revolutionary myth of the times. That myth foresaw the rising of the frustrated industrial proletariat against capitalist exploitation, but some countries on the Continent and elsewhere in the world were thrown into this crisis by different factors: by a general moral and economic despondency that overtook the world after these years of holocaust, by the desire to achieve national independence and consolidation, and by a sense of national humiliation engendered by defeat or disappointed national aspirations.

Although Hungary had emerged as an independent

---

[1] This chapter is based on the transcript of comments at the Berkeley Conference on the Hungarian Soviet Republic.

state from the ruins of an empire, she is not one of the countries liberated from foreign domination but one of the up
till then dominant states that had lost much of their power
in defeat or had been frustrated in their aspirations. In this
sense Hungary falls into the category of Germany and Italy.
Yet while Germany, and to a lesser extent Italy, were fully
developed modern national states, Hungary, with her backward economy and predemocratic political structure experienced a revolutionary upheaval that, in many respects, was
similar to those of the emerging nations in southeast Europe
as well as outside the European continent.

In the previous chapters one comes across sufficient
evidence for this economic and political backwardness and
for the feudal character of society with its castelike social
classes. Hungary was, of course, no longer a full-blown feudal or caste society, but one in which the characteristics of
such a society had more than a lingering effect. For example,
the bourgeoisie was Jewish and as such treated more like a
caste than a class, or the persistence of the traditional idea
that the Magyar nobility was identical with the union, and
that anyone who did not belong to the ruling caste was not
a *bona fide* member of the national community. This was
even true in the working class, which was not a class but
another caste or an estate in the sense that they had fought
for—with more militancy than they are usually credited
with—and won rights in society by compromising in a typ-
ically feudal manner: their rights to participate in matters
of high policy or to interfere with the countryside and the
peasantry, the lowest estate in this hierarchical society.

In a powerful national state and mature industrial society like Germany passionate nationalism and the sense of
national humiliation are not likely to create a revolutionary
impact. They are more likely to create a counterrevolutionary impact. Thus for all the heated debate it generated, na-

tional Bolshevism never made history in Germany or in other western European countries. But in societies yet unintegrated and undeveloped, like Hungary or Turkey, the humiliations inflicted by war were apt to produce a different reaction, and could be regarded as a chance to create a genuinely modern political community, to combine the social and agrarian revolutions with a national one. The Hungarians, like the Turks, the Bulgarians, and the Chinese, wanted to change the condition of their societies, and in order to accomplish it they turned to Russia in a leftist revolutionary upsurge. But at the same time they were also attempting to assert their national identity as Hungarians, Turks, and Chinese and wanted to have rights like any other nation.

Yet, when turning to Russia the Hungarian revolution came under the leadership of people who had too little feeling for the Hungarian reality and who, because of the lopsided development of Hungarian society and their own social background and training, were under the sway of internationalism. They lacked empathy with the problems and sentiments of their own country and had a *Weltanschauung* that not only prevented them from performing the role of national leadership but led to many mistakes, such as their failure to solve the agrarian problem, their intransigence on the religious issue, and even their blunders on the battlefield. These mistakes and the eventual demise of the republic did not represent mere accidents of history; rather they were the consequence of an unbridgeable gap between the adopted ideology of the leadership and the revolutionary situation they tried to exploit.

As Professor Kenez suggested, the mistakes were not only those of the Communists but of the Social Democrats as well. This is an important point and particularly valid with respect to the agrarian question. At the same time one should not underestimate the role and responsibilities of the Communists. While in the course of the revolution Communist influence diminished progressively (and never resulted in organizing an effective party), it was still the formative influence and impetus behind the policies of the regime. Communism, more than social democracy, was the inspiration for the revolution because it represented the hope for Russian involvement and the hope for finding support against Western imperialism. Moreover, the Communists alone were believed to have a program, and if they did not have one in fact, they still had an ideology, a broad outlook that could give rise to a program and determine the general orientation of the revolutionary government. But this ideology lacked the substance that could have transformed the Hungarian revolution into an anti-imperialist movement combining the aspirations of nationalism and social democracy.

Lenin himself had some inkling that the revolutionary situation in eastern Europe had strong national, anti-imperialist and anti-Western elements. Many of Lenin's writings at the time of the Hungarian revolution and the following years show this. But the former prisoners of war whom the Bolsheviks sent home to Hungary were impervious to this element. This was especially true of Béla Kun who today is rated higher than he was by his contemporaries—the result, I think, of the desire to rehabilitate him as a Communist ancestor and Stalinist victim. But although Kun may be a respectable ancestor and was the victim of the purges, his utterances during the 133 days of the republic look just as unimpressive today as they looked at that time. A doctrinaire to boot, bent on following foreign examples in minute detail, he talked about a Brest-Litovsk type peace as early as April 1919 when he had a chance, or so it appeared, to get something better than a Brest-Litovsk—the Smuts offer.

This was not only tactical miscalculation and political insensitivity. Talking of a Brest-Litovsk was not the way to develop an atmosphere for a broad, national revolution. This man, like most Hungarian Communist leaders, was an agitator and nothing more. He was certainly not a political leader, a statesman, or a moral force, but a provincial political primitive who was content to see himself as the manipulator of the Hungarian revolution. In this role he used bribery and tricks instead of appealing to the sentiments in the nation.

Briefly surveying now the ways in which the Hungarian revolution affected international communism, we must start with the question of the party, because it was an important consequence of the Hungarian experience that it transformed and crystallized the Communist concept of political organization.

Strange as it may sound, in 1919 Lenin was not yet a Leninist. Lenin who had a clear concept of what his own party should be, had not yet made up his mind at the time of the Hungarian revolution, about the other parties. He was still undecided whether they should follow the Russian model or ultimately acquire some other shape. This point is frequently overlooked, partly under the influence of Communist propaganda, partly under the impact of Lenin's Communist interpreter Lukács who himself comes from Hungary. Lukács, like almost everybody else, tended to ignore that Lenin's original theory of the party was based on the observation of conditions prevailing in Russia. If one reads *What Is to be Done?* with the eyes of a historian rather than with those of an ideologue, one soon discovers this essential truth. In arguing for a split in the revolutionary movement, for instance, Lenin makes his case in terms of unique Russian conditions in the context of which even the famous argument on trade-union consciousness assumes only secondary importance. Indeed, this last point had been inspired by one of Kautsky's remarks which Lenin quotes on this matter. To be sure, several years before the Hungarian revolution Lenin had already called for a Communist International, but this was merely to rid the masses from the influence of a corrupt leadership and not to combat their false consciousness. At that time Lenin still had faith in the radicalism of the European working classes, and he believed it would be enough to unfold the authentic banner of Marxism to mobilize them for the revolution. For this reason, in 1919 he did not insist on Communist parties of the Bolshevik type. This idea had not yet crossed his mind until after the founding congress of the Comintern, and when the Hungarian party merged with the Social Democratic party he expressed only mild misgivings and let himself be quickly assured that the Hungarians would have a genuine revolutionary party. His change of mind came only after the defeat of the Soviet republic, mainly because he, like the majority of the Soviet and Comintern leaders, was not yet ready to admit that conditions for a purely Communist revolution had not existed in Hungary and found a convenient explanation for its failure in Social Democratic treason. Shortly thereafter Kun and his associates transposed this kind of thinking to the West European scene and concluded that the reason why the world revolution was not advancing quickly enough was not the absence of necessary conditions but the European Communists' lack of the right kind of political organization. Within less than a year after Hungary the Centrist leaders of the French party were barred from the Comintern, the Reformists were thrown out of the Italian party, and the split was made complete on the international level. How large the lessons of Hungary loomed on these occasions and at the second congress of the Comintern is well documented and the subject of a persuasive essay by Professor David Cattell.[2]

As an interesting note to this process of transformation, one may add a few words on the evolution of Georg Lukács' ideas. Lukács was a man of great intellectual compulsion to think out ideas, and he first authored a non-Leninist theory of the party. According to this theory, which had its genesis in the Hungarian revolution, the party was to be self-liquidating and the unification of Socialists and Communists in Hungary represented the first step toward self-liquidation for, in fact, the united party was no longer a party. Even after the defeat, Lukács, in one of his articles published in *Kommunismus,* offered the thesis that the International should seek greater unity in the world movement, and in the process they should treat centralization merely as a *regulative Idee,* a vague organizational standard. Nevertheless in the next few years Lukács went the way of the Comintern and became the protagonist of Leninist organization on the international plane. It was he who subsequently took up the argument on trade-union consciousness and applied it on a world scale, arguing that the revolutionary class consciousness of the workers was really embodied in the centralized party. So here in the higher spheres of philosophical argument one finds the same phenomenon of substituting organization for the correct analysis of a revolutionary situation.

The consequences of the Hungarian defeat for the international Communist movement were not only manifest in the doctrine of splitting and narrowing but also in the personnel used for this purpose—often Hungarian exiles in

---

[2] David Cattell, "The Hungarian Revolution of 1919 and the Reorganization of the Comintern in 1920," *Journal of Central European Affairs,* XI:1 (January-April 1951).

the Comintern. The exiles provide an example for the fact that in an organization that does not want to learn from defeat, nothing succeeds like failure. It is astonishing how people could emerge from a fiasco and become important functionaries on the ground that, having once brought about the contrary, they should know best the virtues of organizational splitting and centralization. In accordance with this principle it was Rákosi who, together with the Bulgarian Kabakchiev, was sent to the Livorno congress of the Italian Communist party in order to split off the reformist minority, and he did so well that he split off the majority of the party. This was justified later by the statement that in order to have a revolutionary party one should, if necessary, split not one but ten times. Again, it was Kun who, together with Paul Vermy, directed the "March action" in Germany with the result of splitting the German Communist party, an act which they subsequently tried to explain by the need of cleaning the German Communist party from the opportunists of the school of Rosa Luxemburg.

The activities of the Hungarian Communist were not popular in all quarters of the Comintern. Thus while the official view was that they were the most experienced functionaries available, others, like Paul Levi, politely suggested that the Soviet leaders could not, after all, be expected to send their best people to serve as emissaries to the foreign parties. Accordingly, the international movement was handed over to people who, in Levi's words, were full of goodwill and eagerness but who turned the international movement into a testing ground trying to show how they would do things if given the chance to seize power again. It was in the same context that Levi coined the phrase of sending "Turkestanis" to run West European workers' parties. The "Turkestanis" were Pogány, Rákosi, and Kun. Today this word still crops up in German but is often misunderstood. What Levi meant was not that Kun and his comrades were Asiatics who did not belong to the European scene, but that they should be sent to Turkestan because there they would do less harm to the international movement. Even less charitable is another view published under the attractive title of *Die Magyarische Pest in Moskau* by an old Hungarian Communist, Heinrich Guttman, who had a grudge against Kun. Writing under the pseudonym Heinrich Unger, Guttman described persuasively how this "plague" had first corrupted communism in Hungary by its Machiavellianism and trickery and how it had then transplanted the same methods into the international movement.

This then takes us back to the note on which I started, for the role that these people were allowed to play in the Comintern reflected the same incongruity that had doomed the Hungarian revolution. It reflected the same messianism and the fundamentally erroneous view that one can substitute organization for objective social conditions and manage a great revolutionary movement by sending out emissaries trained in ideology. This fantasy continued to reassert itself throughout the history of the Comintern and, just as in the Hungarian revolution, was one of the principal factors in bringing about its demise.

Index